Spiritual Authority

The Essential Source of
All Authority is God!

BARRY BORTHISTLE

VIDE

Copyright © 2022 by Vide Press

Vide Press and The Christian Post are not responsible for the writings, views, or other public expressions by the contributors inside of this book, and also any other public views or other public content written or expressed by the contributors outside of this book. The scanning, uploading, distribution of this book without permission is theft of the Copyright holder and of the contributors published in this book. Thank you for the support of our Copyright.

Bible versions used:

New International Version (NIV). Holy Bible, New International Version®, NIV® Copyright ©1973, 1978, 1984, 2011 by Biblica, Inc.® Used by permission. All rights reserved worldwide.

The King James Version of the Bible (KJV). Public domain.

The Message (MSG), Copyright © 1993, 2002, 2018 by Eugene H. Peterson.

Dake's Annotated Reference Bible by Finis Jennings Dake. Copyright 1963 and 1991 by Finis Jennings Dake. Reprinted by permission of Dake Publishing, Inc.

The Amplified Bible (AMP). Copyright © 2015 by The Lockman Foundation, La Habra, CA 90631. All rights reserved.

Vide Press
6200 Second Street
Washington D.C. 20011
www.VidePress.com

PB ISBN: 978-1-954618-52-7
e-Book ISBN: 978-1-954618-53-4

Printed in the United States of America

WHAT IS SPIRITUAL AUTHORITY?
Barry Borthistle
Go to https://growthpartnernetworks.com.
Click on www.solomonsporchteaching.com for podcast information.

YOUR BODY IS GOD'S TEMPLE—AN AMAZING TRUTH
1 CORINTHIANS 6:17-20

"To recognize and receive the wondrous truth of being God's temple is the beginning of walking and living a supernatural life."
—Michael Ellison, author of *10 Habits of Wellness.*

One who learns spiritual authority in his or her life must recognize that the essential source of all authority is God. While many rely on their position granted to them by another human being, spiritual authority comes only from God.

When you walk and live in the incredible truth that you are God's Temple, spiritual authority, which God has promised, becomes life changing.

> To apply God's spiritual authority to your life and circumstances, the one major ingredient you need is FAITH. It is impossible (impotent) to please God without faith. By faith, Noah built a ship in the middle of dry land. By faith, Abraham said yes to God's call to travel to an unknown place that would become his home at age seventy-five. By faith, barren Sarah was able to become pregnant. By faith, George Mueller fed over 10,000 orphans. At this time, England was only looking after 3600 orphans. By faith, Mueller built five large orphanages. By faith, Mueller never asked anybody but God for money and millions of dollars came in.

Remember, nothing is impossible with God (Luke 1:37). The word "nothing" is used seventy-five times in the New Testament and has ten different meanings. The meaning in Luke 1:37 is unique and it is from the word "rhema." Rhema is Greek literally meaning "utterance or saying." So, my translation would read: NOTHING IS IMPOSSIBLE WITH GOD IF IT IS BASED ON HIS SAYINGS (HIS WORD).

Endorsement from Dr. Peter J. Daniels

"Every one of us searching for truth and accountability can dip into the deep well of this extraordinary book with confidence.

I have known this man for many years and observed his ability and steadfast character. With insight and research, Barry takes us behind the curtain of the peripheral into the ancient reliability of meanings and events that nourishes the soul of the reader.

Read this book. It will awaken and satisfy your deepest yearnings. Then send a copy to a friend."

Dr Peter J. Daniels is an international business statesman and world-renowned motivational speaker, and the leading authority on leadership, self-development, and goal setting. He has authored over fifteen books on the "How to" for attaining success from a biblical perspective.

Church leaders refer to him as a "missionary to the business world" and a "merchant of hope", and speak widely of his generosity. Dr Peter J. Daniels has been honored by universities, theological colleges, institutions, governments, businesses, and humanitarian organizations from around the world for his entrepreneurial ability and benevolence.

He has served on international boards with some of the world's greatest intellectual, business, academic, religious, and corporate giants of the twentieth and twenty-first centuries of which his role in the Worldwide Leadership Council, and the Haggai Institute of Advanced Leadership, were prominent.

Honors Received:

Lieutenant Colonel, Aide de Camp, Governor's Staff by Governor George Busbee in the State of Georgia—January 14, 1975.

Kentucky Colonel Commission by Julian M. Carroll, Governor on behalf of the Commonwealth of Kentucky—August 25, 1986.

Honorary Citizen of the City of Austin, Texas, by Frank C. Cooksey, Mayor—February 23, 1987.

Honorary Citizen of the City of Winnipeg, Manitoba, Canada, by William Norrie Q.C., Mayor's Office—October 5, 1987.

Proclamation of Appreciation City of Euclid, Ohio, by David M. Lynch, Mayor—April 20, 1988.

Honorary Ambassador of World Expo 88 Australia by Sir Llewellyn Edward, Chairman of the Board,—1988.

Ambassador to Republic of Ciskei by his Excellency, President Dr. Lennox L. Sebe—May 1989.

Doctor of Humanities by President Gene Moore Jn., March of Faith Bible Institute, Houston, Texas—December 6, 1992.

Ambassador for Life Youth for Christ International by James Groen, President—1995.

Doctor of Letters by President Robert Roberts of Oral Roberts' University, Tulsa, Oklahoma—May 6, 1995.

Proclamation of Appreciation the State of Texas by Rick Green, State Representative—August 5, 2003.

Honorary Doctor of Sacred Letters by Dr. Fabienne N. Smith, President of Jacksonville Theological Seminary—February 7, 2006.

Doctor of Christian Philosophy in Business by Dr. Robb Thompson, President of the International College of Excellence, Tampa, Florida—September 5, 2007.

Master of Christian Leadership by Dr. Robb Thompson, President of the International College of Excellence—September 5, 2007.

Doctor of Humane Letters by President Gene Moore, Sr., of the March of Faith School of Ministry, Texas—April 20, 2008.

Life Achievement Award by Johnathan S. Raymond, President of Trinity Western University Canada, on behalf of the Center of Entrepreneurial Leaders—October 22, 2010.

Historical Events & Involvements:

Became a Christian (1959).

Built the largest Christian Endeavor Youth Group in Australia (1963).

Commenced real estate career (1967).

Decisive legal win for moral decency and community values (1971).

Became director of Peter J Daniels Real Estate (1972).

Personally sponsored and created a significant evangelistic Christian outreach program (1976).

Became Chairman of the Board, Youth for Christ, Australia (1976-1991).

Board member and International Director, Haggai Institute of Advanced Leadership (1977-1991).

Made World Treasurer, Youth for Christ International (1980-1991).

Elected as International Director, Robert Schuller Ministries—"Hour of Power" (1980-1999).

Promoted to Director, International Corporate Holdings (1981-2001).

President and Founder, World Center for Entrepreneurial Studies (1984).

Created a personal tutorial program on business (1988).

Completed authorship of ten books (1989).

Made International Director Worldwide Leadership Council (1993-1999).

Became Chairman, Australia Fair—Strategic Intelligence & Bullion Company (1999).

Joined the Board of Counsel to Anglo Far-East Bullion Company (2001).

Was Chairman of the WCES Foundation (2004).

Founded and became chairman of The Gabriel Call (2005).

Became Chairman of the Board of Counsel Dan El Private Estates (2006).

Conducted over one thousand business seminars in Christian churches globally over the last thirty years (2014).

Now eighty-nine years old, Dr Peter J. Daniels remains happily married to his childhood sweetheart, Robina, and remains an influential leader whose practical wisdom is highly sought after.

Dedication

I have known Michael Ellison for twenty-five years. We first met in the mid-nineties during a visit to my office with his father, Richard Ellison. I was CEO of a large nutritional company. Michael shared his vision for a new concept which I found very interesting but did not fully understand.

Five years later, I received a phone call from Michael inviting me to Phoenix, Arizona, to discuss the possibilities of joining him as cofounder of a new company that would focus on the physical, emotional, and spiritual sides of life. I will admit that I was not very receptive, but my sweetheart, Margaret, who was battling cancer at that time, said, "Barry, this is of God." I accepted the position and began working with Michael on this new company. Sadly, Margaret passed away before we really got started.

I will never forget Michael's opening speech at the Grand Opening of the company in July of 2020. His subject was THE LAW OF RECIPROCITY. His speech had a huge effect on the minds of the people.

Twenty years later, Michael and Margaret were correct and I was wrong. To prove my point, recently I wrote a book entitled *Your Body is God's Temple*.

Having worked with Michael, I have found him to be a man of incredible vision and integrity. I could tell you story after story that would illustrate this statement.

I consider it an honor and a privilege to dedicate my second book, *GOD'S SPIRITUAL AUTHORITY*, to Michael Ellison. Without Michael, I wouldn't have been introduced to the concept that when we live and walk as God's Temple, God is very desirous to give us spiritual authority as long as He receives the honor.

My favorite quote from Michael is, "To recognize and receive the wondrous truth of being God's Temple is the beginning of walking and living a supernatural life."

Thank you, Michael, for your leadership, vision, and friendship.

—Barry Borthistle

Michael Ellison, born in 1946, is a Christian entrepreneur focused on helping people experience greater physical, emotional, and spiritual wellness.

Starting as young as his late teens, he traveled the world to share his faith, spending time in India, Indonesia, Thailand, Japan, and other countries. Seeing the abject poverty of the body and spirit of millions of people, he founded Ellison Media Company, in 1971, specializing in humanitarian and faith-based ministries and conducting services in over 100 countries. Through the years he has helped raise over one billion dollars to help advance the kingdom and to meet the wellness needs of those so impoverished.

DEDICATION

In 1999, Michael Ellison cofounded TriVita, a wellness company, with Barry Borthistle, featuring nutraceutical products, lifestyle recommendations, and a strong spiritual message that your body was created to be God's Temple. In 2013, he established the TriVita Clinic of Integrative Medicine, featuring prevention, early detection, treatment and reversing of chronic related diseases.

Michael Ellison is also author of two books, *10 Keys to Create Wealth & Wellness* and *10 Habits of Wellness*. He is also the founder of House of Giving, a non-profit organization focused on serving those less fortunate.

Michael and his wife, Susan, have been married fifty-five years, having two sons and six grandkids. Together as a family they are serving in their wellness mission and God's calling of helping people experience greater wellness!

Why Do We Need Believers (Spiritual) Authority?
By Andrew Wommack

"Many Christians have adopted a humanistic view of things. They do not realize the spiritual implication behind what is going on in their lives. What I mean by humanistic is that they only look at things on a surface level. They think most everything they encounter on a daily basis is either physical or natural.

The truth is, there is a battle raging every single day in the spiritual realm. That battle is for your heart and the hearts of every other person on Earth.

God is trying to influence people and draw them toward righteousness and toward Himself, so they can live consistent with Him in order for His blessings to be manifest in their lives.

James 4:7-10, 'Submit yourself, therefore, to God, and resist the devil and he will flee from you.'

To win in this war, you must know who you are and the authority you have as a believer."

Remember that you are the Temple of the Holy Spirit and this is why you have the authority as a believer (1 Corinthians 3:16-17 and 1 Corinthians 6:17-20).

Keys (plural) used only twice in the New Testament (keys mean competent authority). Matthew 16:18-19 and Revelation 1:18 (Check it out.)

THIS IS INCREDIBLE:

When Jesus Christ first talked about His Church, He said that it was His Church and He would build it. But to encourage us, He said He would give us the keys to the Kingdom of Heaven (Matthew 16:18-19). The word keys, plural, means "competent authority" and is used in only one other passage (Revelation 1:18).

Jesus was asked the question, "Why do You teach in parables?" He answered the question by saying that He wanted us to know the mysteries of the Kingdom of Heaven (Matthew 13:10-13). John the Baptist announced the arrival of Jesus by saying, "Repent, for the Kingdom of Heaven is at hand." Jesus repeated the exact words in Matthew 4:17.

Contents

*"The Bible was not given for our information
but was given for our transformation."*
—Dwight L. Moody

Foreword... xvii
Chapter 1: The Ultimate Spiritual Authority Is God Almighty (Romans 13:1-7) 1
Chapter 2: The Secret of Spiritual Strength.....................7
Chapter 3: Spiritual Authority Can Only Be Exercised with Faith in God (Hebrews 11:6). Learn about three ways to obtain and exercise faith. Faith is the refusal to panic. —Dr. Martyn Lloyd Jones 17
Chapter 4: Our Spiritual Authority Comes from the Lord (2 Corinthians 10:3-6) 23
Chapter 5: What Are the Conditions of Spiritual Authority? This chapter changed my life (John 15:1-17)..29
Chapter 6: Spiritual Authority Gives You the Power to Become an Overcomer (get the victory) (Revelation 2:7) 35
Chapter 7: Daniel, Obedience and Surrender to the Authority of God (Daniel 6) 45
Chapter 8: God's Condition on How He Will Respond to the Spiritual Authority That He Gives Us at His Temple (2 Chronicles 7:12-17) 49
Chapter 9: Jesus Christ Paid It All 55
Chapter 10: Eight Principles for the Application of Spiritual Authority. 67

Chapter 11: With God's Spiritual Authority Given to Us, We Are Given the Instructions on How to Profit from Rrials (James 1:2-8). Trials teach us who we are. They dig up the soil and let us see what we are made of. —Charles Spurgeon 71
Chapter 12: Haggai—Spokesman for God. 77
Chapter 13: How Shall We Then Live Today? 83
Conclusion 91

Foreword

I just love Barry and Ruth Borthistle. What lovely friends they are!

No question under whose authority they live their lives.

How about you? When confronted with life's conflicts and problems, how do most of us react:

What is this? What's happening? Why me? Why now?

What can I do? What are the facts? What am I missing here?

How do I handle this issue?

How do I manage this?

When all around seems to be falling apart,

When all seems out of control,

When all our efforts appear futile,

Where do we go for help?

Within God's Authority—we pause, we listen, we hear and we must accept that there are forces and guidance and direction available to us even if they are beyond our individual understanding.

What an easy choice for each of us.

We either stand alone in individual weakness. OR,

We walk in God's Authority and accept that counsel, that power and support .

Barry offers us a detailed Biblical road map of why and how we accept God's Authority. All Barry's references are from quoted scripture. Read and research each reference for your own clarity and confidence of purpose.

At conclusion, I wholeheartedly believe—without any question whatsoever—that you too will accept God's Authority as the source of direction in your own life.

—Ken Hayes

CHAPTER 1

The Ultimate Spiritual Authority Is God Almighty (Romans 13:1-7)

Verse 1

"Let every soul be subject unto the highest powers. For there is no power but of God. The powers that be are ordained of God."

Some word definitions:

Soul – (Breath of Life)
Subject – (to obey, submit one's self uto)
Higher – (superior, supreme)

Crucial to Understand:

The word "power" in the Greek is the word "exousia" in verses 1-3 (authority, magistrate).

"Jesus Christ said that all power is given to Him in heaven and earth." —Matthew 28:18.

The other Greek word for power is "dunamis" meaning miraculous power, abundance, might, and wonderful work, and it is the word for the Holy Spirit (Acts 1:8).

"And who lives in you because you are the Temple of the Living God."—1 Corinthians 6:17-20.

"All things were created by the Lord. By Him, for Him." —Colossians 1:15-16.

When Paul refers to governing authorities, he uses a phrase that can best be translated "the Powers that be." He is not just talking about heads of state; he is talking about all levels of authority, all the way down to the local dogcatcher. These are the powers that be, those that exist. He tells us that the thing we must think about these governmental offices is that they are, in some way, brought into being by God Himself.

I often hear people ask, "Which form of government is the best? Which one does God want us to have?" We Americans love to think that democracy obviously is the most God-honored form of government. But I don't think you can establish that from the Scriptures. In fact, the Scriptures reflect various forms of government. So, when you ask, "Which government is the best kind? Is it a monarchy? An oligarchy (i.e., ruled by a few)? Is it a republic? A democracy?" The answer of Scripture is not necessarily any of these. It is whatever God has brought into being. That is best for that particular place and time in history. God has brought it into being.

Now, that government can change. God doesn't ordain any one form of government to be continued forever. If the people grow toward understanding of truth, and morality prevails in a community, the form of government may well take on a democratic pattern. Where truth disappears, governments seem to become more autocratic. But, in any case, the point the apostle makes is that whatever form of government you find, God is behind it. Don't ever think of any state or any government as anything that in itself is opposed to God, because it isn't. that includes Communism as much as any other form of government. That is the clear statement of this passage. I think we have to begin to clear our thinking along that line."

The USA was founded on biblical principles (Isaiah 33:22). Canada was founded on biblical principles (Psalm 72:8). In Chapter 6 of my book *Your Body is God's Temple* you can find a history of these two countries. —Ray Stedman

Verse 2

"Whosoever therefore resisteth the power, resisteth the ordinance of God: and they that resist shall receive to themselves damnation."

Some word definitions:

Ordinance – (institution, arrangement)
Damnation – (Culmination, judge me not, go to law)

When Paul wrote this letter to these Christians, they were living in the capital city of the empire, Rome, itself. Rome by this time had already passed through several forms of government. It had been a monarchy, a republic, a principate, and now it was an empire. Nero had just begun his reign as the fifth emperor of Rome when Paul wrote this letter. What Paul is saying to these Christians is that whatever form of government may be in control, they are to remember that God is behind it.

Not only is God behind the forms of government we have, but he is also responsible for the incumbents, the ones occupying the offices at any particular time. That may be a startling thought for some of us, but that is what this verse says.

Verse 3

> *"For rulers are not a terror to good works, but to the evil. Wilt thou then not be afraid of the power? do that which is good, and thou shalt have praise of the same."*

Here Paul shows the duty of civic rulers. It is not good for government to terrorize men of good deed.

Verse 4

> *"For he is the minister of God to thee for good. But if thou do that which is evil, be afraid; for he beareth not the sword in vain: for he is the minister of God, a revenger to execute wrath upon him that doeth evil."*

This is a very helpful passage, and it says that there are two basic functions of government. Governments are to protect us from evil. That is, they are to preserve the security of people. They are to protect us from attacks from without and from crimes from within. And for that purpose, governments properly have armies and police systems and courts of justice to preserve us from evil in our midst. And then in Verse 5 we have another function of government.

Verse 5

> *"Wherefore ye must needs be subject, not only for wrath, but also for conscience sake"* (KJV).

> *"Therefore, it is necessary to submit to the authorities, not only because of possible punishment but also because of conscience"* (NIV).

Verse 6

"For this cause pay ye tribute also: for they are God's ministers, attending continually upon this very thing." (KJV)

"This is also why you pay taxes, for the authorities are God's servants, who give their full time to governing" (NIV).

Verse 7

"Render therefore to all their dues: tribute to whom tribute is due; custom to whom custom; fear to whom fear; honour to whom honour." (KJV)

"Give everyone what you owe him; if you owe taxes, pay taxes; if revenue, then revenue [Revenue refers to those hidden taxes such as sales taxes, customs duties, etc.] if respect, then respect; if honor, then honor" (NIV).

God's delegated authority does not belong to the person exercising it—that person is just a channel.

Prayer

Our Father, we thank you for these practical words. How eminently practical they are in our lives. How deeply concerned you are even about such matters as this. Forgive us for ever thinking that you aren't concerned. Help us to be good citizens, Lord, but above all, to be faithful to our responsibility to show honor to those to whom honor is due, and respect those who deserve it. Even though they may not personally be men and women deserving of our respect, the office they hold demands it. Thus we pray that we may adorn the doctrine of God our Savior. We ask in your name, Amen.

We are also reminded to pray for those in authority over us. This does not mean you must believe in their political views. The Bible tells us to pray for those in authority. I urge you, first of all, to pray for all people. Ask God to help them, intercede on their behalf, and give thanks for them. Pray this way for kings, all who are in authority, so that we can live peaceful and quiet lives marked by godliness and dignity. This is a great example of spiritual authority as God's Temple (1 Timothy 2:1-3).

CHAPTER 2

The Secret of Spiritual Strength

David Wilkinson

A MESSAGE FOR TODAY

The prophet Isaiah pronounced a woe on Israel: "'Woe to the rebellious children,' says the Lord" (Isaiah 30:1-2, NKJV). The Hebrew word Isaiah uses for "rebellious" means backsliding, stubbornness, and turning away. What, exactly, was God's people turning away from? And what caused their backsliding?

The answer is in the next phrase: "[They] take counsel, but not of Me, and [they] devise plans, but not of My Spirit" (30:1). This means they make their own plans. Simply put, God said, "My people no longer look to me for guidance and counsel. Instead, they lean on the arm of the flesh. Every time they act without seeking me, turning to the world for help, they pile sin upon sin. They've forsaken their trust in my strong arm."

The Holy Spirit gives us strength when we release all our needs into God's hands and trust in his might.

Here, in short, is God's secret to spiritual strength: "Quietness and confidence shall be your strength." The word for quietness in Hebrew means repose, indicating calm, relaxing freedom from all anxiety. This is how God wants us to live as His Temple.

Not many Christians today have this kind of quietness and confidence.

What about your home? Is it a calm, peaceful abode? Or is it a place of doubt, questioning, anxiety, restlessness? Do you run here and there, fretting, "How am I going to pay the bills?" When trouble comes, do you seek God diligently before any other source? Then do you obey everything He tells you to do? Finally, are you still, restful, trusting Him for the result? If so, your home should be one of calm and peace.

Remember, you can do all things (not some things) through Christ who strengthens you (Philippians 4:18). Strength means "to empower" and is a present participle meaning continuous or repeated action.

ISAIAH CHAPTER 30

Verse 1

Isaiah 30:1, "Woe to the rebellious children, saith the Lord, that take counsel, but not of me; and that cover with a covering, but not of my spirit, that they may add sin to sin."

"Not of me...not of my spirit." Hezekiah's advisers urged him to turn to the Egyptians, not to God, for help against the invading Assyrians. Isaiah denounced this reliance on Egypt rather than God, who had forbidden such alliances. The story is told in 2 Chronicles, Chapters 28 and 29.

The children (in verse 1) are those belonging to God. In the physical sense, this is speaking of the descendants of Jacob (Israel). We can see from this that God does not want them seeking counsel from other people. God wants them to seek His counsel.

They are looking for another country (Egypt) to protect them, or be their covering. This is a sin and is just adding this sin to those they have already committed. They should seek forgiveness from God and take counsel of Him. On their behalf, we must remember the way to the Father was closed to them at this time.

The way for the Christians to the Father was opened when the temple veil was torn from top to bottom when Jesus was crucified. In the spiritual sense, here, we can see that God does not want His sons (Christians) to take counsel of the world (Egypt) either.

The Holy Spirit of God is the teacher and guide for the Christian. We are protected by the shed blood of Jesus Christ. Remember, your body is the Temple of God. WHAT AN AWESOME THOUGHT. You can find out more at Biblestudy.org

ISAIAH CHAPTER 30 LISTS SEVEN SINS OF JUDAH AND ALL APPLY TO US TODAY

Seven sins of Judah (verses 1-2):

1. They are rebellious
2. Do not counsel with Jehovah
3. Seek cover (protection) from man
4. Add sin to sin
5. Make alliances with foreigners without inquiring of God
6. Depend upon Egypt for help
7. Trust in the power of Egypt

Sins do not stand alone. When one sin is committed it generally requires others to cover the first one and carry it out (verse 1).

1. Egypt, in Scripture, symbolizes worldly ways.

SPIRITUAL AUTHORITY DEMANDS *WAITING ON GOD*

Why is it important to wait on God?

It is important to note that God does not work according to OUR schedules or OUR lists; He works according to HIS timing and HIS will for us. When we fail to remember this fact, disappointment can set in, which ultimately can lead to anger and resentment; sometimes aimed toward God and this is not a good place to be.

Waiting on God: Why Is It Important to Wait on God?

It is so hard to wait. It even seems impossible sometimes. We make plans, we set goals and we put a time frame for each item on our list and expect each thing to result in a positive outcome. Unfortunately, that's not always how things turn out.

The honest truth is that when we create our goals and our lists, a lot of times we are leaving out the most important factor—and that factor is God. When we leave God out of our goals and lists, honestly, they may go nowhere. There are never any guarantees that it's all going to work out the way we envision it.

—Amy Blossom

ISAIAH 40:31

"But they that wait upon the Lord shall renew their strength; they shall mount up with wings as eagles; they shall run and not be wary; and they shall walk, and not faint."

WAIT (to tarry—to expect to look for with great expectation, with hope) Zechariah tells us that our stronghold is that we are prisoners of (captive or bound by) HOPE—Zechariah 9:12.

Waiting involves the very essence of man. Hope has an eternal mark in the heart of man.

Wait on Purpose

We should wait on the Lord on purpose and make God the focus of our lives. Divorce, addiction, emotional disorders, and criminal records are evidence of lives torn apart because someone decided on purpose to follow some voice other than God's, some counsel other than God's, some plan other than God's.

David wrote, "My soul, wait silently for God alone, For my expectation is from Him. He only is my rock and my salvation; He is my defense; I shall not be moved" (Psalm 62:5,6).

Wait on the Lord with patience, in prayer, and on purpose. He will answer.

Wait with Patience

We should wait on the Lord with patience. When we do not know what to do about something, we should wait. Sometimes we get caught up in just doing something that we neglect to hold still, listen, and know that He is God (Psalm 46:10). When the places of our lives are not fitting together the way we want, we get busy and start trying to force things to work, as Abraham and Sarah did. If we take the time to pursue God's direction and wait for His response, we will get much better results.

THE CHALLENGER OF THE STORM—THE EAGLE

When all other birds try to flee from the storm and hide from its fierceness, eagles fly into it and will use the wind of the storm to raise higher in a matter of seconds. They use the pressure of the storm to glide higher without having to use their own energy (The Eagle Story, Changes For Survival, Ms. Hemi Sudhakar on Instagram).

The eagle can live up to seventy years. But to reach this age, the eagle must make a hard decision in its forties. Its long and flexible talons can no longer grab prey, which serves as food, and its long and sharp beak becomes bent. Its old, heavy wings, due to their thick feathers, become stuck to its chest and make it difficult to fly. Then the eagle is left with only two options: die or go through a painful process of change which lasts 150 days. The process requires the eagle to fly to a mountain and knock its beak against a rock until it plucks it out.

Moral of the story:

Many times, in Order to survive, we have to start a change process. We sometimes need to get rid of old memories, habits, and other past traditions. Only freed from past burdens, we can take advantage of the present.

The Challenge of Change and Change We cannot Dismiss
By Doctor Peter Daniels

1. Recognize that God is the provider and stabilizer in change.
2. Keep your mind on the things you want and also on the things you do not want.
3. Be nice to people.
4. Be patient.
5. Give God the glory.
6. Do not let your mind be deterred by failure. Failure can be the stepping-stones to success.

A FEW FACTS ABOUT EAGLES

1. They mate for Life

Eagles are loyal birds and when they mate it's for life. The only time they tend to find a new partner is if their former partner dies.

2. A Baby Eagle is called an Eaglet

Not only are eaglets the cutest things ever, but they're also stubborn birds. Even though it takes them a while to get the hang of flying, they don't give up.

3. Bald Eagles lose Feathers on Equal Sides to remain Balanced

Bald Eagles rely on their feathers for balance.

So, when they lose a feather on one side, they will lose a matching feather on the other side to balance themselves out.

4. They build their Nests on top of High Cliffs

5. They're a Symbol of Freedom and Peace

6. Eagle's Nests are made out of Sticks, Moss, Plant Stalks, Seaweed, and Lichens

Eagles take pride in their nest. After all, they revisit it every year to have their young. If they like the look of a branch, they will tear it off the tree and use it in their nest. They also use thorns… prickly!

7. Male and Female Eagles are not the same Size

No, actually the female eagle is typically 30 percent bigger than the male. This seems commonplace in the bird world. Some believe that it's so the female can protect her young from foes more efficiently, while the male is said to be a lighter and, therefore, quicker hunter.

8. They're cunning, bold, and intelligent Creatures

These fierce hunters use clever tactics to snare their prey.

They're known to dive in front of the sun during their attack, so their prey is blinded. They don't let their need for food overrule their tactical thinking and cunning abilities.

9. Eagles encourage their Offspring to leave Home when They feel They are Ready

Apparently, the parents will encourage their children to leave home by having them sit on their wings and then the parents will flip them off. If the children do not fly, they
will catch them and do it again. My dear mother, who I love very much, and she loved me, told me: "When you're ready to leave home, don't come back."

THE WORD OF GOD HAS THIRTY-FOUR VERSES ABOUT EAGLES

2 SAMUEL 1:23
Saul and Jonathan were lovely and pleasant in their lives, and in their death, they were not divided: they were swifter than eagles, they were stronger than lions.

APPLICATION:

THE POWER OF STRONG RELATIONSHIPS

PROVERBS 30:18-19
There be three things which are too wonderful for me, yea, four which I know not: the way of an eagle in the air; the way of a serpent upon a rock; the way of a ship in the midst of the sea; and the way of a man with a maid.

APPLICATION:

GOD CREATED EAGLES AND CREATED YOU IN HIS IMAGE AND HIS TEMPLE

JEREMIAH 49:16
Thy terribleness hath deceived. Thee, and the pride of thine heart, O thou that dwellest in the clefts of the rock, that holdest of the height of the hill: though thou shouldest make thy nest as high as the Eagle, I will bring thee down from thence, saith the Lord.

APPLICATION:

YOU MUST HAVE VISION AND PURPOSE

PROVERBS 23:5
Wilt thou set thine eyes upon that which is not? For riches certainly make themselves wings; they fly away.

APPLICATION:

DO NOT PUT YOUR TRUST IN MONEY

CHAPTER 3

Spiritual Authority Can Only Be Exercised with Faith in God (Hebrews 11:6)

Without Faith it is Impossible (Impotent) to Please God (Hebrews 11:6).

1. Faith in God allows us to have forgiveness of sin and to have eternal life (John 3:15-21).

2. Faith permits us to have fellowship with God as there is no darkness in God.

   <u>1 John 1:5-10</u>
   If we repent of sin, God will do four things:

   1. Be faithful to us.
   2. Be just with us.
   3. Forgive our sins.
   4. Cleanse us from all unrighteousness.

3. Faith in the Healing of the Sick (Matthew 9:1-8).

   Jesus exercised His Spiritual Authority because of Faith and God was glorified. Jesus Christ is the total authority.

Prayer for Revelation
Ephesians 1:15-23: This Scripture encourages us to ask God for wisdom and revelation (Verse 17).

God our help and shield with a seven-fold blessing (Psalm 115:12-14).

Summary

Conditions of Spiritual Authority
1. Faith (Hebrews 11:6)
2. Forgiveness and Fellowship (1 John 1:5-10)
3. Give God all the Glory (Psalm 115).

HOW TO OBTAIN FAITH?

- Faith is a gift given at your time of conversion as is Grace (Romans 12:3). We are given a measure, which is a limited portion. It can be as small as a mustard seed (Matthew 17:20- 21). A mustard seed is the smallest seed, but it can grow to a plant of five to six feet high.
- How important is faith in God? Without faith it is impossible (impotent) to even please God (Hebrews 11:6).
- How does our faith increase? We must exercise our faith. Read the story of the centurion's servant in Matthew 8:5-13.
- Faith comes by hearing, and hearing by the Word of God (rhema—revealed; Romans 10:17).

"Have your heart right with Christ and He will visit you often." —Charles Spurgeon

"Faith is the refusal to panic." —Dr. Martyn Lloyd Jones

"Faith without works is dead." —James 2:14-26

Remember, Jesus Christ has all spiritual power in Heaven and Earth, but He wants us to make disciples of all nations (Matthew 28:18-20).

When you obey the Lord, never ask Him to be with you. But praise Him because He is always with you.

Spiritual Authority is claimed by total faith—when all sin in your life has been repented of. Here are some first examples of repentance being required:

John the Baptist—First Sermon Repentance (Matt 3:1-3).
Jesus Christ—First Sermon Repentance (Matt 4:17).
Apostle—First Sermon Repentance (Acts 2:36-39).

HOW LONG DID IT TAKE FOR ISRAEL TO CROSS THE RED SEA?
By Shawn Brasseaux

Remember, it was nighttime when the Jews left Egypt after Passover and during Unleavened Bread. God told Israel that He would smite Egypt's firstborn at "midnight" (Exodus 12:29). Pharaoh called Moses and Aaron in the night, shortly after the firstborn were slain, giving Israel permission to leave Egypt (verse 31). Israel left Egypt sometime after midnight. Exodus 12:42, 51: "*It is a night to be much observed unto the LORD for bringing them out from the land of Egypt: this is that night of the LORD to be observed of all the children of Israel in their generations ... And it came to pass the selfsame day, that the LORD did bring the children of Israel out of the land of Egypt by their armies.*"

Now, Exodus 14:20-23: "*And it came between the camp of the Egyptians and the camp of Israel; and it was a cloud and darkness to them, but it gave light by night to these: so that the one came not near the other* all the night." It was still nighttime when the Egyptian armies tried to attack Israel on the banks of the Red Sea. *"And Moses stretched out his hand over the sea; and the LORD caused the sea to go back by a strong east wind all that night, and made the sea dry land, and the waters were divided. And the children of Israel went into the midst of the sea upon the dry ground: and the waters were a wall unto them on their right hand, and on their left. And the Egyptians pursued, and went in after them to the midst of the sea, even all Pharaoh's horses, his chariots, and his horsemen."*

The Bible says that God drove the waters back "all that night." This seems to be some hours' passage of time (verses 24-27): *"And it came to pass, that in the morning watch the LORD looked unto the host of the Egyptians through the pillar of fire and of the cloud, and troubled the host of the Egyptians, And took off their chariot wheels, that they drave them heavily: so that the Egyptians said, Let us flee from the face of Israel; for the LORD fighteth for them against the Egyptians. And the LORD said unto Moses, Stretch out thine hand over the sea, that the waters may come again upon the Egyptians, upon their chariots, and upon their horsemen. And Moses stretched forth his hand over the sea,* and the sea returned to his strength when the morning appeared; *and the Egyptians fled against it; and the LORD overthrew the Egyptians in the midst of the sea."* Verse 24 says that by *"the morning watch"* (the last portion of the night), the Egyptian armies were still trying to reach the Red Sea and attack Israel. By the *"morning,"* the sea had returned to its normal state and covered the Egyptian armies. The waters went back instantly I am sure, as God's miracles are instant in Scripture (Matthew 8:3; Mark 1:32; Mark 10:52; Luke 4:39; Luke 18:43; John 5:9; Acts 9:18; et cetera), but it evidently took several hours for all of the Jews to cross the Red Sea. It was during this time period of hours that God sustained these walls of water. The waters went back instantly after God let go of them.

True, we do not know how many Jews there were who walked side-by-side across the Red Sea. What we can surmise is that the opening and the closing of the Red Sea happened within the time-span of one night, and thus not days. Exodus 12:29 *("midnight,"* Israel told to leave Egypt) and Exodus 14:27 (*"morning appeared,"* Red Sea covered Egyptians) would give us an estimation of less than six hours, for the Jews to enter the Red Sea and safely pass through to the other shore.

God gave this tremendous Spiritual Authority to Moses because the Heart of Moses was right before God

How wide is the Red Sea where the Israelites crossed?

The parting of the Red Sea not only finalized God's redemption of His people from slavery in Egypt, but it also prefigured the greater spiritual reality of God's redemption of His people from slavery to sin through the work of Christ.

The Red Sea separates the coasts of Egypt, Sudan, and Eritrea to the West from those of Saudi Arabia and Yemen to the East. Its maximum width is 190 miles, its greatest depth 9,974 feet (3,040 meters), and its area is approximately 174,000 square miles (450,000 square km). The Gulf of Suez, the northern end of the Red Sea is roughly where Moses and the Israelites are said to have crossed. Gulf of Suez, Arabic "Khalij As-suways", is the northwestern arm of the Red Sea between Africa proper (West) and the Sinai Peninsula (East) of Egypt. The length of the gulf, from its mouth at the Strait of Jubal to its head at the city of Suez, is 195 miles (314 km) and it varies in width from twelve to twenty miles (nineteen to thirty-two km). It's 230 feet deep.

Moses marched to His own funeral and had God perform it. God was with Moses since he surrendered to Him until the time of his death. Moses was honored again when he and Elijah appeared with Jesus on the Mount of

Transfiguration. Moses had been dead for approximately a thousand years (Matthew 17:1-9).

"You are never too old to dream a dream."
—C.S. Lewis

Moses' dream began at eighty and He lived another forty years.

"Dream a dream so big that, if God is not in it, it will fail."
—Hudson Taylor

CHAPTER 4

Our Spiritual Authority Comes from the Lord

2 Corinthians 10:3-6—The Message

"*The world is unprincipled. It's dog-eat-dog out there! The world doesn't fight fair. But we don't live or fight our battles that way—never have and never will. The tools of our trade aren't for marketing or manipulation, but they are for demolishing that entire massively corrupt culture.*

We use our powerful God-tools for smashing warped philosophies, tearing down barriers erected against the truth of God, fitting every loose thought and emotion and impulse into the structure of life shaped by Christ. Our tools are ready at hand for clearing the ground of every obstruction and building lives of obedience into maturity."

1. Ephesians 6:10-18 The Armor of God
2. 1 Timothy 1:18-20 Wage the Good Warfare
3. 2 Timothy 2:2-5 Be a Single-Minded Warrior
4. Romans 13:11-14 Awake out of Sleep

2 Corinthians 10:3-6

"For though we walk in the flesh, we do not war after the flesh: (For the weapons of our warfare are not carnal, but mighty through God to the pulling down of strongholds;) Casting down imaginations, and every high thing that exalteth itself against the Knowledge of God, and bringing into captivity every thought to the obedience of Christ;

And having in a readiness to revenge all disobedience, when your obedience is fulfilled.

(Obedience cancels disobedience.)

Verse 3

1. WALK—To tread all around, to be occupied—To live used in Galatians 5:16
2. WAR—To serve in a military campaign

- A spiritual confidence used in good sense (1 Timothy 1:18). Loving the world means hating God (James 4:1-20).

3. We are to put on the armor of Light (Romans 13:12-14).

- The Corinthian Christians tended to rely on and admire **carnal** weapons for the Christian battle:
- Instead of the belt of truth, they fought with manipulation.
- Instead of the breastplate of righteousness, they fought with the image of success.
- Instead of the shoes of the gospel, they fought with smooth words.
- Instead of the shield of faith, they fought with the perception of power.
- Instead of the helmet of salvation, they fought with lording over authority.
- Instead of the sword of the Spirit, they fought with human schemes and programs.

The Enduring Word David Guzik

Verse 4

Jesus relied on spiritual weapons when He fought for our salvation. Philippians 2:6-8 describes this: "*who, being in the form of God, did not consider it robbery to be equal with God, but made Himself of no reputation, taking the form of a bondservant, and coming in the likeness of man. And being found in appearance as a man, He humbled Himself and became obedient to the point of death, even the death of the cross.*" **The carnal, human way is to overpower, dominate, manipulate, and out-maneuver. The spiritual Jesus way is to humble yourself, die to yourself, and let God show His resurrection power through you.**

1. "Apart from a mighty awakening and revival in the church, we are fighting a losing battle because we are resisting on carnal levels." (Redpath)
2. **Our spiritual weapons are scorned** by the world but feared by demonic powers. When we fight with true spiritual weapons, then no principality or power can stand against us. "As the spittle that comes out of a man's mouth slayeth serpents, so doth that which proceedeth out of the mouths of God's faithful ministers quell and kill evil imaginations, carnal reasonings, which are the legion of domestic devils, that hold near intelligence with the old serpent." (John Trapp)
3. **Pulling down strongholds: Strongholds** in this context are wrong thoughts and perceptions, contradicting the true knowledge of God and the nature of God. These **strongholds** are expressed in **arguments and every high thing that exalts itself against the knowledge of God.**

4. **Praise God, strongholds** can be pulled down! Clarke recounts with wonder one stronghold pulled down in history: "In like manner the doctrines of the reformation, mighty through God, pulled down—demolished and brought into captivity, the whole papal system; and instead of obedience to the pope, the pretended vicar of God upon the earth, obedience to Christ, as the sole almighty Head of the Church, was established, particularly in Great Britain, where it continues to prevail. Hallelujah! The Lord God Omnipotent reigneth!" (Adam Clarke)

DIVINE, SUPERNATURAL POWER IS REQUIRED TO DEFEAT SATAN'S STRONGHOLDS—OUR ARMOR (Ephesians 6:10-18).

Verse 5

Imagination—thoughts, reasoning.
The Word suggests this contemplation of actions as a result of the verdict of conscience. Translated as "thought" in Romans 2:15.

Knowledge—a seeking to know, an investigation. This usage can be found in Romans 15:13-14, Philippians 3:8, and 2 Peter 3:18.

"For nothing is more opposed to the spiritual wisdom of God than the wisdom of the flesh, and nothing more opposed to His grace than man's natural ability." (Calvin)

Bringing every thought into captivity to the obedience of Christ: to battle against this carnal way of thinking and doing, our *thoughts* must be *brought* captive and made obedient to Jesus.

Verse 6

Speaks of readiness—Being prepared, make ready for revenge—To retaliate, to vindicate, to punish.

Let the Lord repay the vengeance" (Romans 12:19-21).

Disobedience is simply a refusal to hear (Romans 5:19, Hebrews 2:1-4).

Obedience is compliance and submission. Obedience is better than sacrifice (1 Samuel 15:22).

The explanation of godly obedience can be found in verses like 2 Corinthians 7:15, Hebrews 5:8, and 1 Peter 1:2.

"The Scripture was fulfilled" (James 2:23) with Abraham and Sarah. The Law is fulfilled in one word: love (Galatians 5:14).

And being ready to punish all disobedience: Paul was ready to confront the Corinthian Christians, to pull down the strongholds among them if they would not do it themselves. Many commentators think the phrase "among them" is taken from a Roman military court. Paul says, "We are all soldiers together in this battle, and I am ready to bring in some discipline among these troops."

When your obedience is fulfilled: Paul sees no point in coming to confront disobedience until those who have obeyed Jesus have made up their mind to do so. He will give time for those who want to renounce carnal weapons to do so. Then he will come to punish all disobedience of those who will not renounce those carnal weapons.

"Herein the apostle hath set a rule and a pattern to all churches, where are multitudes that walk disorderly; not to be too hasty in excommunicating them, but to proceed gradually; first using all fair means, and waiting with all patience, for the reducing them to their duty, who will by any gentle and fair means be reduced; and then revenging the honor and glory of God only upon such as will not be reclaimed." (Poole)

CHAPTER 5

What Are the Conditions of Spiritual Authority?

In John 15:1-8, God used the vineyard in the Old Testament as a symbol for Israel (Isaiah 5:1-7).

Context: This is the last of the Seven "I AM"

Here are the seven metaphorical "I am" statements found in John's gospel:

1. *"I am the bread of life"* (John 6:35, 41, 48, 51).
2. *"I am the light of the world"* (John 8:12, 9:5).
3. *"I am the door"* (John 10:7).
4. *"I am the good shepherd"* (John 10:11, 14).
5. *"I am the resurrection and the life"* (John 14:6).
6. *"I am the way and the truth and the life"* (John 14:6).
7. *"I am the true vine"* (John 15:1, 5).

The final metaphorical "I am" statement in the Gospel of John emphasizes the sustaining power of Christ. We are the branches, and He is the vine. Just as a branch cannot bear fruit unless it is joined in vital union with the vine, only those who are joined to Christ and receive their power from Him produce fruit in the Christian life.

BECAUSE JESUS CHRIST IS THE VINE AND WE ARE THE BRANCHES, HERE IS WHAT WE MUST DO TO OBTAIN SPIRITUAL AUTHORITY.

Question: What did Jesus mean when He said, "*I am the 'True Vine'*" (John 15:1)?

Answer: "*I am the True Vine*" is the last of seven "I am" declarations of Jesus' recorded only in John's Gospel. These "I am" proclamations point to His unique, divine identity and purpose.

Jesus said, "*I am the True Vine*" to closest friends gathered around Him. It was only a short time before Judas would betray Him; in fact, Judas had already left to do his infamous deed (John 13:30). Jesus was preparing the eleven men left for His pending crucifixion, His resurrection, and His subsequent departure for heaven. He had just told them that He would be leaving them (John 14:2). Knowing how disturbed they would feel, He gave them this lovely metaphor of the True Vine as one of His encouragements.

Who Is the Vinedresser?

"Vinedresser" is just one way to translate the Greek word used by Jesus (Yeshua). It can also mean "Gardener" (NIV), "Farmer" (The Messenger Bible), and "Husbandman" (KJV). It is a generic word for someone who tends plants. Jesus (Yeshua) used this as a name of God the Father when He was teaching about Himself as the True Vine, so the word corresponds to our term "vinedresser." Jesus is the Vine; His Father is the vinedresser who cultivates and prunes the branches so that they bear fruit. Pruning is not cruel; vines thrive when they are heavily pruned each season.

WHY IS PRUNING A TREE NECESSARY?

If a tree is allowed to grow out of control, it may lead to improper weight distribution over the crown or other parts of the tree. This can cause a strain on the roots and even restrict nutrients to vital parts of the tree if not addressed in a timely manner. Overweight branches also may compromise branch structures which can lead to weak branches that are prone to breakage. As the tree ages, these problems may result in a shorter lifespan and a poorly performing crown.

John 15:7 – The All-Intensive Condition of Prayer

1. If—begins with us. It is our choice. There are over 1,500 ifs in the Bible. In this verse, there are three ifs. Verses 6, 7, and 10. There are eight ifs in the chapter. Eight is the number of new beginnings in the Bible.
2. Abide (to continue, to dwell, to remain, to tarry). Abide is mentioned seven times in John 15, and seven is the number of perfection.
3. Two kinds of branches—This is the principle of a wine orchard. Key point: fruit must be produced.
4. We are purged through the Word of God as all Scripture is given by the inspiration of God (2 Timothy 3:16-17). Inspiration means God-breathed.
5. Jesus repeats that He is the True Vine, and we can do nothing without Him. This is where faith must come in. How to obtain faith? Look back to Chapter 3.
6. To obtain God's Spiritual Authority: It begins with us and then Jesus as the Vine gives us His instructions to obtain Spiritual Authority.
7. *If ye abide in me and my words.* In Greek, there are two meanings of the word *word*. Logos meaning "written" and Rhema meaning "revealed.

The word here is "rhema." The Spiritual Authority that the Vine gives us is to ask what ye will and it will be done. "Ask" is an imperative, which means "a command for doing something."

This is when the Christian life gets exciting.

Unlike the Old Testament, where the Holy Spirit did not dwell within the Temple, or unless God anointed a man or woman. Question: Are you abiding in the rhema Word of God?

"What we need is for Him to fill our minds and hearts with His thoughts. Then His desires will become our desires flowing back to Him in the form of prayer. James 4:3 confirms this: "You ask and do not receive, because you ask amiss, that you may spend it on your pleasures." If we ask amiss, we are certainly not asking according to His will, and we will not receive.

But doesn't Jesus say in John 16:23, "Whatever you ask the Father in My name He will give you"? He most assuredly does, but we still do not have a *carte blanche*. To ask God for anything in the name of Jesus Christ, it must be in keeping with what He is. To ask in Christ's name is to ask as though Christ Himself were asking. Therefore, we can only ask for what Christ Himself would ask. It is therefore necessary to set aside our own will and accept God's. Jesus says in John 8:29: "And He who sent Me is with Me. The Father has not left Me alone, for I always do those things that please Him." If we do as Jesus did, we are sure to receive answers as He did. He adds in John 11:41-42: "Father, I thank you that You have heard Me. And I know that You always hear Me."

We must come away with the realization that prayer is not dictating to God, but a humble and heartfelt expression of our attitude of dependency and need. Because of this, the one who truly prays is submissive to God's will, content with Him supplying his need according to the dictates of His sovereign pleasure. The result of this, combined with the infusion of God's attitudes and thoughts as we draw near to Him, will work to create us in His image." —John W. Ritenbaugh

WHAT ARE THE CONDITIONS OF SPIRITUAL AUTHORITY?

The Rhema Word of God is the helmet of salvation and the sword of the spirit (Ephesians 6:17). The Rhema Word of God is the Word of Faith (Romans 10:8).

The Rhema Word of God endures forever (1 Peter 1:25).

ALWAYS REMEMBER, GOD IS HOLY AND SOVEREIGN.

Did you know that the Holy Spirit does thirty-three things for us?

God's Word is alive through the power of the Holy Spirit.

"If the Holy Spirit was removed from the early church, 95 percent of what was occurring would stop. If the Holy Spirit was removed from the church today, everything would continue."—AW Tozer

This is who we are in Jesus Christ:

1. We are a peculiar (special) people (Titus 2:14).
2. We are the bride of Christ (Ephesians 5:22-23).
3. A holy nation (1 Peter 2:9).
4. Temple of the Holy Spirit (2 Corinthians 6:17-20).
5. We are saints (1 Corinthians 1:2).
6. We are preserved blameless at His coming (1 Thessalonians 5:23).
7. A royal priesthood (1 Peter 2:9).
8. We are called living stones (1 Peter 2:9).
9. We are called a spiritual house (1 Peter 2:5).
10. A people of God (1 Peter 2:9).

Jesus Christ is the Cornerstone (1 Peter 2:6-7).

> The Holy Spirit prays for us with love you cannot imagine (Romans 8:39).

CHAPTER 6:

Spiritual Authority Gives You the Power to Become an Overcomer

Luke 10:17-20

Verse 19: This is very important. Jesus gave the spiritual authority—power (exousia—to exercise authority).

The second time power (dunamis) is mentioned. This is the word used for the Holy Spirit. Acts 1:8 is the promise made by Jesus Christ Himself, which is also translated as "miracle" in Acts 8:13, Acts 19:11, 1 Corinthians 12:12.

Jesus said, in Matthew 13:11, that we will be given to know the mysteries (secrets) of the Kingdom of Heaven.

The Mysteries of the New Testament

The words "mysteries" or "secrets" are mentioned twenty-seven times in the New Testament. Listed below are fifteen individual mysteries. What is a mystery: The Greek definition is "musterion", which means imposed silence, secret. It is only a New Testament word.

The mysteries of God can only be understood by believers through the power of the Holy Spirit, according to Colossians 1:24-29.

1. Mysteries of the Kingdom of Heaven (Matthew 13:11).
2. Mysteries of the Kingdom of God (Luke 8:10; Mark 4:15; Mark 9:1; 1 Corinthians 4:5; Revelation 10:7).

3. Mystery when Israel accepts Christ as Messiah (Romans 15:24-26).
4. Mystery of salvation (Romans 16:25-27; Ephesians 3:3,4,9; Ephesians 6:19; Colossians 4:9).
5. Mystery of the wisdom of God (1 Corinthians 2:7).
6. Mystery of the Second Coming of Jesus Christ (1 Corinthians 15:51-52).
7. Mystery of the will of God (Ephesians 1:9).
8. Mystery of Christ and the Church, His Bride, in the context of marriage (Ephesians 5:32).
9. Mystery of Christian fellowship in the context of knowing God and Christ (Colossians 2:2).
10. Mystery of lawlessness in context of great apostasy in end times (2 Thessalonians 2:7).
11. Mystery of faith (1 Timothy 3:9).
12. Mystery of godliness (1 Timothy 3:16).
13. Mystery of seven stars (Revelation 1:20).
14. Mystery of Babylon (Revelation 17:5, 7).
15. The mystery of Jesus Christ (Colossians 4:3).

One day all mysteries will no longer be in effect (Revelation 10:7). Why is this so important? Because 1 Corinthians 4:1, 2 said so.

"Christians today need to be informed about the various Mysteries because ALL the deeper matters of Scripture are predicated upon understanding them." —John Malone

Who is an overcomer? The word means "to get the victory or to conquer."

1. Jesus Christ overcame the world (John 11:33).
2. We are all overcomers if the Word of God abides in us (1 John 2:13-15).

3. The word overcomer appears in all seven churches in Revelation: Chapter 2:7, 2:26, 3:5, 3:12, 11:2, 17:2. Jesus is telling us to remain steadfast in Him regardless of what we're going through.

Luke 10: Jesus gives us ten instructions for Spiritual Authority

1. Verse 3: Go—this is foundational.
2. Verse 3: Be wary.
3. Verse 4: Live by faith.
4. Verse 4: Be focused.
5. Verses 5 and 6: Extend your blessing.
6. Verse 7: Be content.
7. Verse 7: Receive your due.
8. Verses 7 and 8: Be flexible.
9. Verse 9: Heal the sick.
10. Verse 9: Proclaim the Kingdom.

ARE YOU LIKE ME? DESPERATE FOR GOD?

Jesus mentions the Church for the first time in the New Testament in Matthew 16:17-19.

The word "church" (A Calling Out) is used about eighty times. Also translated "assembly" three times.

Verses 18 to 19—Jesus said He would build His Church (Acts 2:37-47).

And He will give us the keys to the Kingdom of Heaven (Spiritual authority).

Matthew 16:18,19 (A more accurate translation of this verse from the Greek), "And I will give thee the keys of the kingdom of the heavens. And whatever thou shalt bind on the earth shall be as having been bound in the heavens; and whatever thou shalt loose on the earth shall be as having been loosed in the heavens." This is the first time the *ekklesia*, frequently translated "church" is mentioned in the entire New Testament. A distinction must be made between the Church referred to in verse 18, being the earthly side of God's kingdom but not the only side. The kingdom of the heavens in verse 19, on the other hand, refers to both the Church on Earth, the kingdom of God within the believers (Luke 17:21), and also the kingdom of heaven as a far larger implication than the Church on Earth. The teaching here is that those things which are conclusively decided by the King in the kingdom of heaven.

Reference is made to the acts of persons and not to the decisions concerning persons by the church as an ecclesiastical or organizational body. The Church here is the body of believers themselves. We as believers can never make conclusive decisions about things but can only confirm those decisions which have already been made by the King Himself as conclusive in the general context of His kingdom both on Earth and in Heaven. See Matthew 18:18, where the same two verbs, "to bind" and "to loose", are said to be possessed by all the disciples. See also John 20:23.

The two verbs *dedemenon* and *lelumenon* are both perfect passive participles which should have been translated respectively as "having been bound" and as "having been loosed" already in the heavens. Believers on Earth can only confirm what has already taken place in Heaven.

The Keys to God's Heart

1. Repentance.
2. Obedience.
3. Faith.
4. Praise and worship.

This is very interesting: The first sermon preached was on repentance!

SPIRITUAL AUTHORITY GIVES YOU THE POWER

1. John the Baptist. (Matthew 3:1-3).
2. Jesus Christ (Mathew 4:17).
3. The Apostle Peter in the first Church (Acts 2:38).
4. What Are the Keys of the Kingdom?

> The Keys to the Kingdom of Heaven
> are Spiritual Authority.
> —Gotquestions.com

The biblical passage that makes reference to the "keys of the kingdom" is Matthew 16:17-19. Jesus had asked His disciples who people thought He was. After hearing several of the more popular opinions, Jesus aimed His question directly at His disciples. Peter, responding for the twelve, acknowledged Jesus as the Christ, the Son of the living God. After this great confession, Jesus replied, "Blessed are you, Simon Bar-Jonah! For flesh and blood has not revealed this to you, but my Father who is in heaven. And I tell you, you are Peter, and on this rock I will build my church, and the gates of hell shall not prevail against it. I will give you the keys of the kingdom of heaven, and whatever you bind on earth shall be bound in heaven, and whatever you loose on earth shall be loosed in heaven."

Keys are used to lock or unlock doors. The specific doors Jesus has in mind in this passage are the doors to the Kingdom of Heaven. Jesus is laying the foundation of His church (Ephesians 2:20). The disciples will be the leaders of this new institution, and Jesus is giving them the authority to, as it were, open the doors to heaven and invite the world to enter. At this point it is important to understand how, biblically speaking, one enters the Kingdom of Heaven.

Jesus said that, unless one is born again, he will not see the Kingdom of Heaven (John 3:3). One is born again as the Holy Spirit works through the Word of God to bring about new life in a dead sinner. The content of the message is the substitutionary death of Christ and His subsequent resurrection (Romans 10:9-10). So the faithful preaching of the gospel is the key to the kingdom.

In Matthew 16:19, Jesus is specifically addressing Peter, so it is significant that, in the book of Acts, Peter figures prominently in the "opening of doors" to three different groups of people so they can enter the Kingdom. In Acts 2, it is Peter who preaches in Jerusalem on the Day of Pentecost; about three thousand Jewish people are saved that day. Peter's preaching had "unlocked the door" of heaven for the Jews. Later, in Acts 8, the Samaritans believe the gospel and receive the Holy Spirit; again, Peter (and John) was present for this event. Peter had "unlocked the door" for the Samaritans. Then, in Acts 10, Peter brings the gospel to a Roman centurion's household, and they, too, receive the Holy Spirit. Peter had "unlocked the door" for the Gentiles. The "keys" that Jesus had given them worked in each case.

Of course, keys can be used to lock doors as well as open them. Part of the gospel message is that faith is necessary. Without faith in Christ, the door to heaven is shut and barred (see John 3:18). As the apostles preached the gospel, those who responded in faith and repentance were granted access to the Kingdom of Heaven; those who continued to harden their hearts and reject the gospel of God's saving grace were shut out of the Kingdom (Acts 8:23).

The context of Matthew 16 also refers to a "binding and loosing." To better understand this concept, we turn to Matthew 18:15-20, where Jesus gives the guidelines for church discipline, using the same "binding and loosing" language we find in Matthew 16. The apostles were not to usurp Christ's authority over individual believers and their eternal destiny, but they were to exercise authority to discipline erring believers and, if necessary, excommunicate disobedient church members. Based on God's Word, believers today can declare an unrepentant sinner to be unsaved (bound) and a repentant believer in Jesus Christ to be saved (loosed).

The binding or loosing, based on one's rejection or acceptance of the gospel, reflects heaven's perspective on the matter. In heaven, Christ ratifies what is done in His name and in obedience to His Word on Earth.

God's will is that sinners be granted access to heaven through the righteousness of Christ. Consider Jesus' warning to the Pharisees, "But woe to you, scribes and Pharisees, hypocrites! For you shut the kingdom of heaven in people's faces. For you neither enter yourselves nor allow those who would enter to go in" (Matthew 23:13). If the gospel message is distorted or ignored, or if unrepentant sin is not adequately disciplined, the doors to the Kingdom of Heaven are being shut in people's faces.

Conclusion

Spiritual Authority is the proof of the New Birth (1 John 5:2-5). Loving God and keeping His commandments is the price of our salvation, and that we love others.

What does the Bible say about being an overcomer?

The term "overcomer" comes from the Greek *nikaw*, "to conquer, prevail, triumph, overcome." This verb is found twenty-eight times in twenty-four verses in the New Testament. This presupposes and calls attention to the presence of war, contests, battles, and conflicts in man's struggle with evil.

The Bible sounds a definite call to God's people to overcome a multitude of things: Satan, sin, the world, the flesh, and the fallen human life. Those who love the Lord Jesus sense a corresponding echo within, calling them to live an overcoming life.

JESUS SAID: "In the world ye shall have tribulation: but be of good cheer I have overcome the world" (John 16:33).

The word "keys" (plural) is mentioned only two times in the New Testament. The first is in Matthew 6:19 and the second is Revelation 1:18. Check this out!

God Rewards His Overcomers

"He who has an ear, let him hear what the Spirit says to the churches. To him who overcomes I will give some of the hidden manna to eat. And I will give him a white stone, and on the stone a new name written which no one knows except him who receives it."
—Revelation 2:17

Overcoming is a present participle – means a continuous or repeated action.

Listen to the voice of the Holy Spirit (Revelations 2:17).

"I will give him hidden manna"

1. Hidden—to conceal, to keep secret.
2. Manna—the only place used in the New Testament The food God provided for Israel. The overcomer reflects the Life of Christ (Revelation 2:17).
3. White stone—It is known as a victory stone.

"These were known to the ancients as victory stones. Also in ancient times they meant pardon and the evidence of it. Judges had white and black stones. If a black one was given the criminal was condemned: If a white stone he would be pardoned. Conquerors in the public games were also given white stones with their names in them, which entitled them to be supported the rest of their lives at public expense. Perhaps all three things are meant by the white stone to the overcomer." Overcomers are followers of Christ who successfully resist the power and temptation of the world's system. An overcomer is not sinless but holds fast to faith in Christ until the end. He does not turn away when times get difficult or become an apostate. Overcoming requires complete dependence upon God for direction, purpose, fulfillment, and strength to follow His plan for our lives (Proverbs 3:5-6; 2 Corinthians 12:8-10).

Amazing conclusion: Jesus was asked why He spoke in parables. His answer: so that we would know the mysteries of the Kingdom of Heaven (Matthew 13:11). Again, this is why he gave us the keys (which means competent authority to gain spiritual authority).

CHAPTER 7

Daniel, Obedience and Surrender to the Authority of God

Book of Daniel Chapter 6 Summary

Daniel means "God is my judge."

- Daniel is able to retain his high position, even though the Babylonian Empire has just fallen to pieces. He continues to serve as one of Darius the Mede's top three men—presidents who supervise the one hundred and twenty satraps that help govern the kingdom (a "satrap" is basically a state governor).
- But the other two presidents and the satraps all get jealous of Daniel. He's been doing so good that Darius is planning to make him his number one president, ruling over everyone else except for the king.
- The satraps can't find anything to discredit Daniel with in his own life, since he's a pretty clean-living and incorruptible guy. So they devise a plot.
- The satraps go to Darius and start to kiss up to him. They convince him to sign a document ordering everyone to pray to him and worship him—and only him—for thirty days, or else they'll be thrown into a den full of lions.

How many Traps would a Satrap Trap if a Satrap could trap Traps?

- Daniel pays no attention to the new rule and continues to pray to God at his window facing Jerusalem.
- The satraps go to Darius and tell him what Daniel is doing. But the king really likes Daniel and makes every effort he can to save him. Still, the satraps tell him that he can't change his own laws.
- So, Darius orders Daniel thrown into the lion's den—though, before it happens, Darius tells Daniel that he hopes God can save him. After Daniel is put inside, the den is sealed over with a giant boulder.
- After heading home, Darius refuses to eat. He fasts and is unable to sleep, as well.

Satraps Entrapped by Their Own Trap

- The next day, Darius heads down to the den to see if God saved Daniel. He has! Daniel is fine and answers the king when Darius calls to him. Daniel explains that God's angel showed up and made sure the lion's mouths stayed shut. So, Daniel is saved, and Darius allows him to be taken out of the den.
- But the king punishes the people who conspired against Daniel—not only the satraps and presidents, but their wives and children are chucked into the lions' den. The lions start to devour them and crunch their bones before they even hit the floor.
- Like Nebudchadnezzar before him, Darius issues a proclamation, telling everyone that they need to respect and fear Daniel's God. He pays tribute to God for saving Daniel and says that God's kingdom will outlast all others.

- The chapter ends, stating that Daniel went on to do pretty well for himself, both during Darius' reign and that of the next king: Cyrus.

8 Facts About Daniel

1. Daniel is renowned for His wisdom and intelligence (Daniel 1:20). His specialty is as a dream interpreter (Daniel 2:27; Daniel 5:15-17).
2. Daniel's righteousness is of legendary status (Daniel 1:8).
3. Daniel's ministry spanned the entire seventy-year captivity (Ezra 1:1-4).
4. Daniel introduces us to the only two angels named in the Bible: Gabriel and Michael (Daniel 8:15-19; Daniel 9:21-27).
5. Daniel wrote the prophetic book of Daniel through the power of the Holy Spirit. Because Daniel understood the SPIRITUAL AUTHORITY that God gave him, his prophetic words are coming true in this age in which we live. Simply amazing (Daniel 12:4).
6. Daniel prayed three times a day with windows open, and on his knees in faith.
7. About 2600 years ago, the Holy Spirit inspired Daniel to tell us that in the End Times travel will increase. Since then, we have gone from walking to Outer Space.
8. Knowledge will increase. Up until 1900, knowledge increased about every 100 years. By World War II, it was every twenty-five years. Then to two years, then to eighteen months, and heading toward twelve hours. This is all according to IBM.

CHAPTER 8

God's Condition on How He Will Respond to the Spiritual Authority That He Gives Us at His Temple

"To recognize and receive the wondrous truth of being God's Temple is the beginning of walking and living a supernatural life!" —Michael Ellison

The Glory of the Lord will enter just as it did with Solomon's Temple when the People obeyed the Lord.

2 Chronicles 6:1-11—Result of Solomon's prayers: Divine acceptance and God's Glory entered the Temple. King Solomon prayed for twelve things at that time.

Why is Our Body, as the Temple of God, So Important Today?

Because man himself was created to be the temple or dwelling place of God, sin ruined the temple. God is now restoring man through redemption to be His temple, indwelt by the Holy Spirit of God (1 Corinthians 3:16, 17; 6:16-20). Believers, both individually and corporately, constitute the temple of God today.

Because the temple was a symbolic and typical representation first of Christ (John 2:19-21), and secondly of the Church (1 Corinthians 3:16,17; 6:16). Believers are spoken of as "living stones", being built into a "spiritual house" as the "temple of the Holy Spirit" (1 Peter 2:5-9). The temple was a prophetic structure. Immaterial truth was hidden in material form to help us understand. The material structure represented spiritual insights.

Because, as will be seen, the earthly temple was a shadow of the Heavenly Temple. Both the Tabernacle of Moses and the Tabernacle of David were earthly shadows of heavenly things. The same is true of the Temple of Solomon. The true Temple is eternal and heavenly. John saw "the Temple of the Tabernacle of the testimony in heaven opened" (Revelation 15:5; 11:19). The things built on earth were built after the "pattern of things in the heavens" (Hebrews 9:23-28).

Both Moses and David, who received the revelation of the Tabernacle and Temple in heaven actually saw the same truths.

—Kevin J. Conner

(And not only so, but we also joy in God through our LORD JESUS CHRIST. By whom we have now received the ATONEMENT.)

Solomon's Temple Prayer

Solomon the King knelt down with arms lifted up to heaven in front of all his people. It is important to remember that when God asked Solomon what he wanted, **Solomon responded by asking for wisdom** (1 Kings 3:3-13). God has extended the same offer to us (James 1:5-6).

Solomon prayed for twelve things (2 Chronicles 6):

1. God's faithfulness—verses 14-16
2. God's continued faithfulness—verses 16-17
3. God's omnipresence—verse 18
4. Plea for answer to prayer—verses 19-21
5. Plea for just judgment—verses 22-23

GOD'S CONDITION ON HOW HE WILL RESPOND

6. Plea for forgiveness of sin—verses 24-25
7. Forgiveness and rain from heaven—verses 26-27
8. Plea for God's help in a time of pestilence, war, and sickness—verses 28-31
9. Blessings on Gentiles who are seeking God—verses 22-23
10. Plea for God's help in war even if no sin had been committed—verses 34-35
11. Plea for help in war when sin had been committed—verses 36-39
12. Plea for God's continued presence and blessing—verses 40-42

2 Chronicles 7:12-22—God appeared to Solomon a second time, twenty years after the dedication of the Temple (2 Chronicles 8:1).

2 Chronicles 7:13-15—God obviously knew the people would not be obedient after Solomon's dedication prayer. This is God speaking to us today. In verse 13, God says "if" three times, which means it is His choice. There are 1,522 instances of the word "if" in the Bible.

- "If I stop the rain…"
- "If I command locusts to devour the land…"
- "If I send pestilence…"

Today, according to PBS, 2021 could be the driest year in the last thousand years.

Today, there are billions of locusts destroying the food supply in parts of Africa and East Asia and are affecting twenty-three other countries, according to the BBC.

Pestilence is a contagious, infectious disease greatly affecting us today in the form of COVID-19.

Verse 14—To me, this is one of the most incredible verses in the Bible because it is directed to us today. "If [our choice] my people who are called by name will do four things…"

1. Humble themselves, which means to bend the knee. It is used in 2 Chronicles 34:27. Spurgeon said voluntary humbleness is what God is looking for (that's what Solomon did).
2. Pray. Pray means to make supplication, to ask for. There are at least twelve preparation steps for prayer in order for God to even hear our prayer (details to follow). Two of the most important are repentance (1 John 1:5-10; five "ifs" in that chapter) and forgiving others (Matthew 6:14-15).
3. Seek my face. Seek me means to search out, to worship, or to request (Psalm 80:7, 19).
4. Turn from your wicked ways. Turn means return to the starting point or to relinquish. Solomon used the word turn three times in his prayer (2 Chronicles 6:26, 37, 42).

If we do these three things, here is God's promise to us:

1. I will hear you from Heaven (Hear means to give attention).
2. I will forgive your sin as far as the East is from the West (Psalm 103:12).
3. Heal your land, which means to mend like a physician, to repair thoroughly, DIVINE INTERVENTION. The word heal is also used in Isaiah 53:2-5 in the context of our salvation. Isaiah 53 is considered by many to be the most important chapter in the Old Testament.

Human repentance and obedience can change the mind of God.

1. Noah (Genesis 6:1-8).
2. Moses and the golden calf (Exodus 32:9-14).
3. Amos the prophet (Amos 7:3-6).
4. Jonah (Jonah 3:10).

The word heal is also used for physical healing in 2 Chronicles 30:20.

CHAPTER 9

Jesus Christ Paid It All

Life is in the blood (Leviticus 17:14)

"Without a doubt, the blood of JESUS CHRIST is the most precious gift our Heavenly Father has given to His church. Yet, so few people understand its value and virtue. Most people seldom, if ever, enter into the power of that blood." —David Wilkinson

Isaiah 53:4-6 to You with Love

Communion as a Celebration

1. Celebrating the provision of the forgiveness of sins (John 3:16-18).
2. Celebrating the return of the Bridegroom (Jesus Christ) for His Bride (the Church) (1 Thessalonians 4:13-18).

Excerpts from *THE POWER OF THE HOLY COMMUNION* by Joseph Prince:

What Is Holy Communion?

The Holy Communion, known also as the Lord's Supper, represents the greatest expression of God's love for His people.

Two items are used in the Holy Communion—the bread which represents Jesus' body that was scourged and broken before and during His crucifixion, and the cup which represents His shed blood.

When Jesus walked on earth, He was vibrant and His body was full of life and health. He was never sick. But before Jesus went to the Cross, He was badly scourged by the Roman soldiers and His body was torn as He hung on the cross.

At the cross, God also took all our sicknesses and diseases and put them on Jesus' originally perfect and healthy body, so that we can walk in divine health. That is why the Bible says, "by His stripes, we are healed." In Luke 22:20, Jesus tells us that the cup is the "new covenant of My blood," and the Apostle Paul tells us that the blood of Jesus brings forgiveness of sins (Colossians 1:14; Ephesians 1:7).

The word "heal" in Isaiah 53:5 and in 2 Chronicles 7:14 has exactly the same meaning (divine intervention).

1. Salvation is divine intervention.
2. Physical or mental healing is divine intervention.
3. Healing our land is divine intervention.

Why do Believers partake of the Holy Communion?

Besides being born again in Christ, a healthy body and mind are the greatest blessings anyone can have. Holy Communion is God's ordained channel of healing and wholeness.

On the night that He was betrayed, Jesus ate His last supper with His disciples. Knowing what He would accomplish through His sacrifice, He instituted the Holy Communion (Luke 22:14-23; I Corinthians 11:17-34).

His loving instruction is that we are to remember Him as we partake of the Holy Communion. Jesus wanted us conscious of how His body was broken for our wholeness and His blood was shed for the forgiveness of our sins. And whenever we partake in this consciousness, we "proclaim the Lord's death till He comes" (1 Corinthians 11:26).

Today, when we partake of the bread, we are declaring that Jesus' health and divine life flows in our mortal bodies. When we partake of the cup, we are declaring that we are forgiven and have been made righteous. Jesus' blood gives us right standing before God, and we can go boldly into God's presence (Hebrews 4:16).

How do I partake of the Holy Communion?

Before you partake, remember that the Holy Communion is not a ritual to be observed, but a blessing to be received.

Preparation for Communion is Very Important

1 Corinthians 11:25—Remembrance (Recollection)
Verse 28 Examine—to test
Verse 30—If we do not obey, consequences are severe.

1. Weak, which means strength-lessness or impotent.
2. Sickly, weak or infirm sickness.
3. Sleep, a judgment on spiritual laziness.

- Jesus Christ is now our High Priest (Hebrews 2:17, 4:14-16, 7:26, 10:19-25).
- The Blood of Jesus is greater than Abel's, and Christ is now the Mediator (intercessor) by the sprinkling of His blood (Hebrews 12:23, 24).

"In scripture, the blood is spoken of in two ways:

1. Blood shed
2. Blood sprinkled." —David Wilkinson

Where did the Blood of Jesus Christ go when He died?

Where is the blood of Jesus today? Charles Spurgeon, prince of preachers, tells us: "When we climb into heaven itself…We shall not have gone beyond the influence of the blood of sprinkling: nay, we shall see it [the Blood] where more truly present than in any other place. 'What!' you say, 'the blood of Jesus in Heaven?' Yes! Let those who talk lightly of the precious blood correct their view ere they be guilty of blasphemy" (CH Spurgeon, "The Blood of Sprinkling" Metropolitan Tabernacle Pulpit). Again, Spurgeon said, "The Lord has gone there [to Heaven] and has sprinkled His blood on the mercy seat." When did Jesus sprinkle His blood on the heavenly Mercy Seat? According to Dr. DeHaan, MD, Jesus Christ ascended to His Heavenly Father before anyone could touch Him (John 20:11-18). The key is verse 17.

The Holy Spirit tells us that the New Covenant could not take place until the blood of Jesus Christ entered the heavenly Holy Place. Then Jesus became our High Priest and our sins were forgiven (Hebrews 9:6-11 23-28; 10:19-25). Key point: as believers, we now have access to our High Priest, Jesus Christ, 24/7 (Hebrews 4:12-14).

Seven ways Jesus Christ shed His Blood

Jesus spilled His blood seven ways—seven is the number of completion.

1. Sweat drops of blood while praying: Luke 22-39-46.
2. Slaps to the head: Matthew 26:67.
3. Beard pulled out: Isaiah 50:5-6.
4. Back whipped with lead and glass: Isaiah 53:3-5 (thirty-nine times).
5. Crown of thorns: Matthew 27:27-31.

GOD'S CONDITION ON HOW HE WILL RESPOND

6. Nailed to the Cross: John 19:17-27. Crucifixion was considered the most brutal and shameful way to die.
7. Blood poured out of His side: John 19:34. The water likely came from the pericardium, which is a sack around the heart and lungs.

Surely he hath borne our griefs, and carried our sorrows: yet we did esteem him stricken, smitten of God, and afflicted. But he was wounded for our transgressions, he was bruised for our iniquities: the chastisement of our peace was upon him; and with his stripes we are healed. All we like sheep have gone astray: we have turned every one to his own way; and the Lord hath laid on him the iniquity of us all.
—Isaiah 53:4-6

Heal means to cure, to make well, divine intervention. The word heal here is the same as in Chronicles 7:14: "Heal our land."

Hold the Blood

- All the "mountains" in your life are prime candidates for holding the Blood of Jesus!
- There is one caveat to this: the Blood is not effective IF there is an open or hidden SIN in your life. In other words, the SPIRITUAL BLOCKS in your life MUST be dealt with to be successful in applying the Blood of Jesus to your situation.
- The spiritual blocks are unforgiveness, disobedience, rebellion, fear, anxiety, doubt, unbelief, sin. 1 John 1:5-10. There isn't any darkness in the Lord (Matthew 6:14-15—Suggested reading before Communion).

- Why? Satan has a clear-cut legal case to keep the victory from you. But more importantly, the Lord is hurt by it!
- God is not obligated to bring victory to the rebellious or the disobedient. Get the sin out of the camp!

There is a difference between blood shed and blood applied. Applying the Blood of Jesus (Google David Wilkerson sermon, April 15, 1996, "The Precious Blood of Jesus Christ")

- "The Blood of Jesus Christ is the most powerful, the most precious and the most valuable substance in the entire universe" —David Wilkerson.
- It ALONE has the power to save to the uttermost, to heal and to deliver. It has the power to transform a life no matter how far gone they may be.
- There is NO OTHER WAY to be saved from sin and a devil's hell except through THE blood of the lamb of God, Jesus Christ!
- "The Blood of Jesus Christ is regarded by God as the most important agent given to us (1 Peter 1:19)."—Charles Spurgeon.
- When God told Moses to strike the blood of a perfect lamb around the doorpost (strike means to apply), the blood would be useless unless it was applied. We don't need to plead the blood because we already have the blood of the perfect Lamb of God, Jesus Christ, which can be applied to your life.

Taking Communion daily or as often as You decide

This prayer can be applied to any situation in your life:

"Father, I come before you in the Name of Jesus Christ, who shed His precious blood that I might have the victory in EVERYTHING that Satan throws at me! I bring my [child] before you now and claim them for the Kingdom of God! I refuse to let Satan take them away from me and You!

By an act of my FAITH, I draw a bloodline with the precious blood around my child's spirit, soul, and physical body! I draw the bloodline around their education, performance, friendship, and everything that concerns them! I know Father, that You will perfect their life! Satan, I remind you of the blood of Jesus that covers my house, business, marriage, family! You cannot cross this bloodline in the Name and the authority of Jesus Christ of Nazareth, who defeated you by His death and resurrection! I bind you from operating against my child any further in the Name of Jesus!

Father, I thank you for the victory! I thank you that my child is Your child! I thank You that their spiritual eyes are being opened to Your goodness! I now stand in FAITH and I BELIEVE and TRUST You for my child's life!"—Apply the blood of Jesus Christ to any situation in your life.

Remember: There is Power in the Blood of Jesus Christ

In the Old Testament, the priest had to inspect the perfect lamb for four days and then wash his hands.

Pilot examined the perfect lamb, Jesus Christ, and then declared, "I find no fault in him" (Matthew 27:24).

ATONEMENT: In the Old Testament, this word was used seventy-five times. It means to be pardoned for one year. The day of atonement was Yom Kippur.

Atonement in the New Testament is used only one time (Romans 5:11). It means restoration to divine favor. Think about it!

POWERFUL CONCLUSION

1. Jesus Christ was tempted in every way and is now our very compassionate High Priest; Hebrews 4:14-16.
2. The Holy Spirit makes intercession for us; Romans 8:26,27
3. Jesus Christ also makes intercession for us to the Father (Romans 8:31-37; Hebrews 7:20-28). This is the greatness of our High Priest. Before you apply the blood of Christ to any situation, please make certain that the communication line is open to heaven.

Two vital principles:

1. Repent of sin (1 John 1:5-10).
2. Forgive others (Matthew 6:14-15).

Amazing Truths

1. After the Passover, God led about two million people out of Egypt with silver, gold, and not one person who was sick (Psalm 105:37-45).
2. We are reminded about the vital importance of preparing for Holy Communion (1 Corinthians 11:24-34).
3. Israel had four days to inspect the Lamb (Exodus 12). The lambs for sacrifice were bred and born in Bethlehem. Pilot inspected our perfect lamb JESUS CHRIST and could find no fault in Him (John 18:38).
4. Paul reminds us in 1 Corinthians 11:23-26 that as often as we observe Communion, we do remember what Jesus Christ has done for us. Consider daily or weekly Communion.

Remember the promise in Isaiah 53, "The chastisement of peace was upon Him."

Closing Thought—King Hezekiah

2 Chronicles 29-32: Hezekiah inherited a wicked Israel from his father. The first thing he did was repair the Temple (we are now God's Temple—1 Corinthians 3:16-17). Then the King restored Passover which had not been celebrated for over 200 years. After the passover, God healed the people (2 Chronicles 30:32). There is healing in Communion (2 Corinthians 11:17-34).

The precious blood of Jesus Christ is the most powerful agent in the world. Remember that the blood of Jesus Christ is now in the Holy Place in Heaven (Hebrews 9:11-28; 10:19-25).

Application for us today:

1. The first Passover (Exodus 12). Verses 3 to 5: "The lamb must be without blemish." John the Baptist called Jesus the Lamb of God (John 1:29).

    Verses 21 to 24 in Exodus: the Lord instructed Moses to take hyssop and strike the blood from the basin around the lintel and doorposts.

    Key word: Strike means to apply. In other words, if the blood remained in the basin, it would be totally useless.

    Hyssop represents transferring the blood sacrifice to the sinner. In Psalm 51:5-9, David says, "Purge me with hyssop and I shall be clean."

    John 19:28-30: the last thing that Jesus Christ did before He died on the cross was to accept vinegar or sour wine on hyssop and, by doing so, accepted the sins of the world (1 John 1:5-7).

Exodus 12 contains the instructions for the Passover where, if Israel followed God's instructions, He would pass over the house instead of killing the firstborn.

1 Corinthians 11:17-34 are the instructions given to us for the celebration of Communion. Like Israel, if we follow the instructions to accept Christ as Savior, death will pass over us and we will spend eternity in the New Jerusalem.

The Symbolism of Hyssop

Why did God tell Moses to apply the blood with hyssop? Hyssop has the properties of assisting with:

1. Intestinal pain.
2. Loss of appetite.
3. Anti-inflammatory properties.

Today, hyssop is used as a fragrance for soap and cosmetics.
Hyssop is used in the Bible ten times in the Old Testament and two times in the New Testament and is always connected to:

1. Healing, which includes cleaning with blood (Numbers 19:18-22).
2. God instructed Moses to apply the blood from the basin to the door with hyssop. If the blood was left in the basin it would have no value (Exodus 12:21-22).
3. David said, "Purge me with hyssop and I shall be clean and white as snow" (Psalm 51:7).
4. The very last thing that Jesus Christ did before He died was to take vinegar from hyssop and then said His last three words: IT IS FINISHED (John 19:28-30).

What is finished? In the Bible, hyssop has a symbolic meaning of transferring the blood of the sacrifice to save the sinner.

REJOICE: It is finished because Jesus Christ paid it all.

I STRONGLY SUGGEST THAT YOU TURN TO PAGES 71-75 AND PLACE THEM IN YOUR BIBLE FOR YOUR DAILY READING.

CHAPTER 10

Eight Principles for Application of Spiritual Authority

1. James 4:7-12: Submit to God.
Submit means to obey, to subdue. Submit is an imperative—which means it is a continuous, repetitive action.

2. Jesus Christ—Submit all to God the Father that God the Father may be all in all.
1 Corinthians 15:27-28 speaks more on this.

3. Marriage—Husband and wife are to submit to each other in the fear of God.
Look to Ephesians 5:21.

4. Spiritual Authority is claimed by total faith in God (Hebrews 11:6).

Biblical Example The Story of Noah

God was sorry He had created man because of sin. To show His love He gave mankind 120 years to repent (Genesis 6:10).

But Noah found grace in the eyes of the Lord—we are given grace (Romans 12-3). God then asked Noah to build an ark on dry land which took about a hundred years.

Noah obeyed God even though it had never rained (Genesis 2:5) and the first rain came after Noah was in the ark (Genesis 7:4).

The Story of Jonah (Jonah 3:10)

God saw their works, that they turned from their evil way, and God relented or changed his mind of the evil that He said He would do unto them, and He did it not.

1. **God responds to four main things: repentance, obedience, faith, and worship.**

2. **Abraham and Sarah traveled and moved to a new land.**
   (Genesis 12:1-4)
   Story of the obedient faith of Abraham can be found in Genesis 12:1-25; Romans 4:1-12; Hebrews 11:8-12.
   Because of the faith of Abraham, the promises made to Abraham are ours today (Galatians 3:26-29).

3. **We submit to Jesus Christ for salvation.**
   According to Romans 10:9-13.

4. **We submit to God when we meditate on His Word day and night.** (Psalm 1:1-3) There are nine blessings from meditating on the Word of God.

5. **Submitting to God's Authority in Government.**
   (Romans 13:1-7) Details in Chapter 1.

What does it mean to submit to God? The biblical concept of submission is to **place oneself under the authority of another.** When we submit to God, we give our lives to His authority and control. In what ways can we submit ourselves to God? One way to submit to God is through salvation.

There are over 1500 "ifs" in the Bible.

EIGHT PRINCIPLES FOR APPLICATION OF SPIRITUAL AUTHORITY

Spiritual Authority can only be exercised if we obey what Jesus Christ said were the two greatest Commandments (Matthew 22:36-40; Mark 12:28-31).

1. To Love God with all of your soul and mind.
2. To Love your neighbor as yourself.

CHAPTER 11

With God's Spiritual Authority Given to Us, We Are Given the Instructions on How to Profit from Trials

How to apply Spiritual Authority to trials (The world cannot provide this kind of advice.), according to James 1:2-8.

Verse 2:

COUNT (to lead the way/to have rule over/to be chief)

The Jewish-culture believer believed that the more trials you have the closer you are to God. Paul, in 2 Timothy 3:12, teaches that trials are part of a godly life.

JOY (Calm delight/cheerfulness/exceeding gladness)

The joy with which we endure trials in the present is a signal of hope for future relief.

FALL INTO (to fall into something that surrounds you/ to light upon you)

Like the story of the Good Samaritan, you may not even have caused the trial. Read the Good Samaritan story (Luke 10:25-37). Remember, Jesus taught what the two greatest commandments are:

1. To love God with all of your heart/soul/mind. Remember your body is the Temple of the Holy Spirit who lives within you (1 Corinthians 3:16-17, 6:18-20).
2. To love (agape) others as you love yourself.

DIVERS (various in character)

TEMPTATIONS (adversity, trails with a beneficial purpose and effect)

The Lord knows how to deliver the godly out of trials and temptation (1 Peter 2:7-9). The Lord knows, which means to understand or hold divine knowledge. See Matthew 6:8, which says that God knows what we need before we do.

Verse 3:

KNOWING THIS (to understand/to realize).

THE TRYING OF YOURSELF (trying means to test).

What is faith? "Faith is the substance of things hoped for, the evidence of things not seen" (Hebrews 11:1). How important is faith? "Without faith it is impossible (impotent) to please God but He rewards those who diligently seek Him" (Hebrews 11:6). Faith is a gift that God gives us, but we have to use it to make it grow (Romans 12:3).

PATIENCE (abiding under).

Patience perfects the Christian character, so let patience have her perfect work. Patience is the ability to persevere through increasing levels of trials.

Verse 4:

PERFECT WORK.

"But let endurance and steadfastness and patience have full play, and do a thorough work, so that you may be perfectly and fully developed lacking in nothing."
—The Amplified Bible

WANTING NOTHING—Jesus promised in Matthew 6:24-34 where He tells us to put God's Kingdom first and all will be given to us.

"Worry is a sin and can produce anxiety/fear/disease and even mental illness."
—The Dake Annotated Reference Bible

"What happens when you worry? Your mind and body go into overdrive as you constantly focus on WHAT MIGHT HAPPEN."
—Web MD

Verse 5:

WISDOM/IF

There are about 1600 "ifs" in the Bible and the word usually means that someone has to make a decision. God asked King Solomon what he wanted, and Solomon's answer was found in 1 Kings 3:3-15.

"Lord, give your servant an understanding mind."

God asks us the same question with a promise and instructions:

- We are to ask (which means call up or to do something).
- Giveth: Giveth is a present participle which means continual or repeated action with no indication of timing. In other words, it's up to God.
- Liberally (unconditional supply).

Verse 6:

FAITH

Faith is our choice because if we do not ask in faith, we are like a wave in the sea.

"Ask" is a present imperative which means a command to do something, including continuous or repeated action.

Matthew 7:7-8 tells us to keep on asking, keep on seeking, and keep on knocking.

Verse 7:

If we do not follow the principles of verses 2-6, we will receive nothing from the Lord. WHY?

Verse 8:

Because we are double-minded (two-spirited), vacillating in our original purpose, and we are unstable (restless in our ways) (James 4:1-10). Loving the world means hating God. (Very important to understand: verses 2-4 must be obeyed before you can ask for the wisdom of God.

Now it is time for Self-Examination.

Here is a checklist of qualities in your life that will assist you in assessing whether you are obeying and trusting the Lord, especially through trials:

Positive	**Negative**
➤ Courage	➤ An Uncaring Heart
➤ Boldness	➤ Pride
➤ Patience	➤ Arrogance
➤ Steadfastness	➤ Temper
➤ Perseverance	➤ Controlling Spirit
➤ Humility	➤ Know-it-all
➤ Self-control	➤ Discouragement
	➤ Gossip
	➤ Blaming Others/ Not Forgiving

CHAPTER 12

Haggai—Spokesman for God

Haggai challenges Israel after the exile to remain faithful to their God after the exile to remain faithful to their God and rebuild the temple.

The people of Israel were conquered by Babylon because they broke their covenant with God through idolatry and injustice. The book of Haggai was written seventy years after this prophesied exile and recounts the experience of a small group of Israelites, led by Joshua and Zerubbabel, who had returned to rebuild Jerusalem.

After thousands of years, the book of Haggai remains largely unique among the books of Old Testament prophets for one key reason: the people of Judah listened! Haggai's message to rebuild the temple was passionate, simple, and straightforward (Haggai 1:8). No one could mistake whether or not his direction had been followed—the results would be evident for all the people to see. Through the physical act of rebuilding the temple, the people began to indicate a shift in their spiritual lives: from devotion to self toward devotion to God.

First message:
Rebuild God's Temple
Rebuke Reflection
Repentant response
"I will bless you!"
"I have chosen you!"
Rebuild God's Temple
"I am with you!"

Second, Third, and Fourth Messages:
Encouragement and Hope
"Take courage!"

Haggai knew that the people were struggling because they had not obeyed God promptly. They had put their own desire for comfortable homes ahead of their desire to complete the task God had assigned to them.

We must learn from the Jews' mistake to prioritize God's work and respond quickly to the assignments He gives us. Good intentions will not get the job done; we must act. The book of Haggai reminds us to obey without delay, when God asks us to do something for Him.

(1:4) **Paneled houses** refers to the upper-income homes of Zerubbabel and Joshua. Their homes had expensive wood interior paneling to cover the stones on the walls and ceiling (similar to Solomon's palace in 1 Kings 7:3,7). Why were these leaders spending lavishly on their own homes and giving no priority to building God's house?

(1:5) **Consider your ways** is a call for serious thinking on the decisions the people were making and what these choices said about their priorities. Would they take the easy way out, or would they follow God's ways?

(1:6) **God was not blessing** the work of their hands. There must be a theological reason why these people were not receiving what they needed.

(1:8) God's desire was that the people **build the temple** and give priority to worshiping God. Whatever one does, God should always **take pleasure in it** and **be glorified** by it. These are two practical theological criteria that people can use to evaluate their life and set new priorities. Jesus set the example, for everything He did was aimed to please God (John 8:29). The reason He came to earth was to glorify the Father (John 12:27-28).

The first chapter of Haggai introduces us to a group of people who had ignored an instruction from God. He had told them to rebuild the temple eighteen years earlier, but they told themselves it was not the right time to do it. Instead of rebuilding God's house, they built their own houses during those eighteen years and experienced fruitlessness and frustration as a result. They found themselves in desperate circumstances. They never had enough money. Things were not working out for them. Whatever they did gain, they quickly lost.

God spoke to them through the prophet Haggai and said, "Consider your ways" (1:7). In other words, "Look at your situation and ask yourselves why you are in such dire straits; it is because you are trying to take care of yourselves instead of obeying Me and working together to provide something for everyone. It will not work!"

Selfishness did not work for the people of Haggai's day, and it will not work for us today. It stops up every avenue of blessing that would otherwise flow into our lives. (Please consider this! God is very interested in all of us considering our ways today.)

Selfish people are quite miserable and usually think if they could just get what they want, they would feel better. Satan has them on a treadmill of striving to make themselves happy and never succeeding.

Why is Haggai so important? After thousands of years, the book of Haggai remains largely unique among the books of Old Testament prophets for one key reason: the people of Judah listened. Haggai's message to rebuild the temple was passionate, simple, and straightforward.

Spiritual transformation happens when God stirs up people's hearts, convicts them of sin, and emboldens them to act in faith.

> *"So the Lord stirred up the spirit of Zerubbabel the son of Shealtiel, governor of Judah, and the spirit of Joshua the son of Jehozadak, the high priest, and the spirit of all the remnant of the people; and they came and worked on the house of the Lord of hosts, their God."*
> *—Haggai 1:14*

Second, Third and Fourth Messages:
Encouragement and hope

"Take courage" "I will bless you!"
"I have chosen you!"

Key point: God has always had a remnant (Romans 11:5). He even has one in the tribulation period (Revelation 11:13, 12:17, 19:2).

Putting the Rhema Word of God to work in Spiritual Authority

Haggai 2:3,4 really are verses about dealing with change. When changes come into church, finances, health, or any other area of life, some people are unhappy. This is easy to understand. They will say, "I wish we could go back to the way we did it before," or "I liked the old way better." How do you handle change in your life, your church or your country?

Pray for your leaders, that they will have wisdom in making decisions concerning the church and continue to be actively involved in the life and ministry of the church remembering that God is with you.

Haggai 2:15-19 illustrates the importance of making God's purposes for your life is top priority. Without priorities, it is difficult to live with any sense of purpose or to accomplish much. What are your priorities in your life?

Haggai was an older man looking back on the glories of his nation, a prophet with a passionate desire to see his people rise up from the ashes of exile and reclaim their rightful place as God's light to the nations.

Haggai challenged the discouraged people in Jerusalem to examine the way they were living and to set new priorities that would please God. They must remember that God was with them; He controled their future and wanted His people to be holy.

Since the Temple of Solomon had been destroyed, God wanted a second temple to be built so He could communicate with His people. So, He chose Haggai to challenge the people to build the second Temple.

Message and Purpose: Through his messages, Haggai tried to persuade his audience to glorify God by rebuilding the Temple. He argues that one should not focus on one's own needs (1:4), be discouraged because the Temple was not as glorious as Solomon's (2:3), be unclean and unholy (2:10-14), or feel useless and powerless (2:20-23).

Haggai's message was that if the people would place God at the center of their lives, they would realize the blessings that God had in store for His people. We need to realize that we are now His people.

More and more glory. In Haggai 2:9, God promises that the glory of the latter house will be greater than the glory of the former temple.

Do you know that you and I are the Temple of God today (See 2 Corinthians 6:16) and that God's glory (His manifest excellence) is upon us? Just as the temple in Haggai would increase in glory, so you and I also increase in glory as we grow in God. The glory we had in the past (the former glory) is not as great as what we have today or will have tomorrow. In 2 Corinthians 3:18, Paul states that God changes us "from one degree of glory to another." In other words, the changes in us personally, as well as in our circumstances, take place in degrees.

When we obey, God promises us peace (Shalom) by Doug Hershey.

"Shalom" is taken from the root word shalam (Hebrew) which means "to be safe in mind, body, or estate." It speaks of completeness, fullness or a type of wholeness that encourages us to give back—to generously repay something in some ways.

Haggai's encouragement to rebuild the temple in the face of the Jews' neglect brings to mind the apostle Paul's exhortation to Christians to build our lives on the foundation of Jesus Christ.

God's Promised Blessing (Haggai 2:18-19).

"Consider now from this day and upward, from the four and twentieth day of the ninth month, even from the day that the foundation of the Lord's temple was laid, consider it.

Is the seed yet in the barn? Yea, as yet the vine, and the fig tree, and the pomegranate, and the olive tree, hath not brought forth: from this day will I bless you.

Apparently acts of confession and spiritual revival took place at this time. Because of this change, God could richly bless their future crops and fill their empty granaries.

CHAPTER 13

How Shall We Then Live Today?

1. Occupy or do business until He comes (Luke 19:13).
   Key Point: retirement is not a biblical idea. Retirement was introduced in 1880 in Europe when the average age of death was sixty-five.

   Suggested reading: *As Long as I Have Breath* by Bruce Gordon, Focus on the Family.

2. Watch and pray.
   Key Point: watch, keep awake, be alert, spiritual alertness (Matthew 26:41-42).

   "Watch and pray." The word translated "watch" means "to have the alertness of a guard at night." A night watchman must be even more vigilant than a daytime guard. In the daytime, danger can often be spotted from a distance. But at night, everything is different. A night watchman must use senses other than sight to detect danger. He is often alone in the darkness and without the defenses he would otherwise employ. There may be no indications of enemy attack until it happens, so he must be hypervigilant, suspecting it at any moment. That is the type of watching Jesus spoke about.

3. Give thanks to God (1 Corinthians 15:57, 58).
   Key point: be steadfast, fixed, moral, settled, immovable—firm in your biblical worldview; abounding better, exceed, excel, over and above, in the work of the Lord.

A knowledge of biblical prophecy will help us prepare and be ready for the return of Jesus Christ (1 Thessalonians 4:13-18). We are blessed if we read, hear, and obey prophecy (Revelation 1:3).

4. Live in faith.
   Key point: without faith it is impossible (impotent) to please God (Hebrews 11:6). Be faithful.

5. Love.
   Love (agape) is the greatest gift (1 Corinthians 13:1-13) (See David Wilkerson's sermons "An Eclipse of Faith" and "The Unreasonableness of Faith").

"Faith is the refusal to panic."—Dr. Martyn Lloyd Jones

Love is patient and kind. Do everything in love. There is no fear in love (1 Corinthians 13).

6. Comfort and edify one another (1 Thessalonians 5:1-11).
   Key point: comfort (encourage) each other and edify or build each other up. Especially in light that the day of the Lord will come as a thief with sudden destruction.

7. Remember your redemption draws near (Luke 21:25-28).
   Key point: our attitude and lifestyle should be looking up, to be elated. Lift up means to be poised and ready because the coming of the Lord is near.

8. Keep an eye on Israel (Genesis 12:1-3).

Biblical prophecy is approximately 30 percent of the Word of God. If we know this, we will be blessed by God. This is the first of seven blessings in Revelation. You are blessed if you read it, hear it and obey it (Revelation 1:3). Seven is God's number.

1. Revelation 1:3
2. Revelation 14:13
3. Revelation 16:15
4. Revelation 19:9
5. Revelation 20:6
6. Revelation 22:7
7. Revelation 22:14

All seven of these verses are about our future.

9. Repent

Whatever happened to repentance? Jesus Christ Himself said of this mission in Matthew 9:13 and Luke 13:3. Jesus' Gospel was all about repentance; Matthew 3:1-2 John the Baptist preached about repentance. First sermon of Jesus Christ preached repentance (Matthew 4:17). First sermon in the Church—Peter's Repentance (Acts 2:38). Without repentance God cannot forgive us (Matthew 6:14-15). There is no darkness in God.

Five "ifs" in (our decision) Acts 2:36-47.

The early church had as its foundation an explosive growth following repentance.

10. What should the attitude of the Church be today? Is there hope? Praise God—YES! 2 Chronicles 7:12-22 key verse is verse 14.

The context in which the Lord gives us these instructions is in the vital importance of obedience as Solomon had just dedicated the temple where God dwells. Today, God dwells in the temple of the believers (2 Corinthians 6:16-19).

Is there hope? Praise the Lord—YES!

When we repent, our attitude will demonstrate our sincerity. The hardest part of repentance is changing the behavior that originally propelled the sin.

Key point: God responds to:

1. Repentance (1 John 5-10).
2. Obedience (Four great examples: Hebrews 11:4,7,8,11).
3. Faith (Hebrews 11:6).

Key point: Be conscious of your sin daily and remember our gracious Saviour will forgive. He will cast your sin as far as the east is from the west (Psalm 103:12).

11. Continue to witness for the Lord (Acts 1:8, Matthew 28:16-20).
    Key point: "The balance of expectation (that Jesus Christ could come at any moment) and participation (serving Him faithfully until He comes) is what the Christian life is really all about."—Ed Hinson.

12. The world is literally held together by the Word of God, according to John 1:1-3. The original word here is logas.

Be a person of prayer
The Holy Spirit intercedes for us to Jesus Christ (Romans 8:26-27) who then intercedes for us to the Father (Romans 8:34; Hebrews 7:25). Remember to please, and not to grieve, the Holy Spirit because you are the Temple of the Holy Spirit (Ephesians 4:28-32).

Behavior Follows Belief in All Areas of Life

"Behold I will do a new thing, now it shall spring forth, shall you not know it? I will even make a way in the wilderness, and rivers in the desert."
—Isaiah 43:19

How Now Shall We Live? Quotes

"Christians who understand biblical truth and have the courage to live it out can indeed redeem a culture, or even create one. This is the challenge facing all of us in the new millennium."
—Charles W. Colson, *How Now Shall We Live?*

"Capitalism is astonishingly efficient at generating new wealth, but it operates beneficially only when the market is shaped by moral forces coming from both the law and the culture—derived ultimately from religion."
—Charles W. Colson, *How Now Shall We Live?*

"(Phil. 4:8). Notice that Paul doesn't limit that principle to spiritual things; he says if anything is excellent. Paul is telling us to train our tastes to love the higher things—things that challenge our mind, deepen our character, and foster a love of excellence—and this includes the music we listen to, the books and magazines we read, the films we watch, the forms of worship we employ."
—Charles W. Colson, *How Now Shall We Live?*

The Rise and Decline of Western Thought and Culture
Quotes by Francis A. Schaeffer

"Drawing upon forty years of study in theology, philosophy, history, sociology and the arts, Dr. Schaeffer contemplates the reasons for modern society's sorry state of affairs and argues for total affirmation of the Bible's morals, values, and meaning."

"We must realize that the Reformation world view leads in the direction of government freedom. But the humanist worldview with inevitable certainty leads in the direction of statism. This is so because humanists, having no god, must put something at the center, and it is inevitably society, government, or the state."

"If man is not made in the image of God, nothing then stands in the way of inhumanity. There is no good reason why mankind should be perceived as special. Human life is cheapened. We can see this in many of the major issues being debated in our society today: abortion, infanticide, euthanasia, the increase of child abuse and violence of all kinds, pornography ... the routine torture of political prisoners in many parts of the world, the crime explosion, and the random violence that surrounds us."
 —*Whatever Happened to the Human Race?*

"The basic problem of the Christians in this country in the last eighty years or so, in regard to society and in regard to government, is that they have seen things in bits and pieces instead of totals."
 —*A Christian Manifesto*

"When a man comes under the bloom of Christ, his whole capacity as a man is refashioned. His soul is saved, yes, but so are his mind and his body. True spirituality means the lordship of Christ over the total man." —*Art & The Bible*

"Truth carries with it confrontation. Truth demands confrontation; loving confrontation, but confrontation nonetheless." —*The Great Evangelical Disaster*

"To recognize and receive the wondrous truth of being God's Temple is the beginning of walking and living a supernatural life."
—Michael Ellison

God has given each of us gifts of faith and grace (Romans 12:3). Jesus promised us his peace through the power of the Holy Spirit (John 14:7).

(Dietrich Bonhoeffer, the great German pastor, theologian, martyr, was asked in 1943 how it was possible for the Church to sit back and let Hitler seize absolute power? His firm answer:
"It was the teaching of cheap grace.

Cheap grace is the preaching of forgiveness without requiring repentance, baptism, without church discipline, communion without confession, absolution without personal confession. Cheap grace is grace without discipleship, grace without the Cross, grace without Jesus Christ." **—Dietrich Bonhoeffer)**

We live in a time, and culture, that not only teaches cheap grace but praises it.

Conclusion

All the glory, honor, praise, and thanksgiving must go to the only one true God

Psalms 115 speaks of Glory.

What is glory? Glory

Honor. Praise. Presence. Credit. Admiration. Holy. The word *glory* takes on a variety of meanings. When was the last time you longed after the glory of God? When was the last time you gave God the glory? Have you ever thought about the Lord's glory showing through you?

Glory Belongs to God

"Not unto us, O Lord, not unto us, But to Your name give glory, Because of Your mercy, And because of Your truth."
—*Psalm 115:1*

The psalmist reminds us that we are to give God the glory or praise because He is God, not a lifeless idol (vv. 2-8). We are to give Him glory because of the blessings He has given us (vv. 9- 15) and because He created the earth for us to enjoy (v. 16).

The Glory of God's Presence

Sometimes the word glory actually refers to the presence of the Lord, as when Moses and Aaron said to the Israelites that "in the morning you shall see the glory of the Lord" (Exodus 16:7).

David wrote, "The heavens declare the glory of God" (Psalm 19:1) and begged to see God's glory. When Solomon dedicated the temple, God's glory came in the form of a cloud and filled the house (2 Chronicles 5:13, 14).

When the angel announced the birth of Jesus to the shepherds, the glory of the Lord shone around them (Luke 2:9). The Lord's Prayer ends with "For Yours is the kingdom and the power, and the glory forever" (Matthew 6:13).

God's Glory in Christians

Ever since the Holy Spirit fell upon those first believers in the Upper Room, God's glory has been manifested through Christians. Jesus said, "Let your light so shine before men, that they may see your good works and glorify your Father in heaven (Matthew 5:16)." Our capacity to reflect God's glory is based upon the degree of our submission to the Holy Spirit and the Word of God. We are to serve the Lord with gladness and let people see His mercy and His love by the way we live, work, and worship—not for our glory but for His. "By this My Father is glorified, that you bear much fruit; so, you will be My disciples" (John 15:8). Peter says believers who never saw Jesus rejoice with "joy inexpressible and full of glory" (1 Peter 1:8).

God's Glory to Come

We know that Jesus sits at the right hand of God and will soon come back "in a cloud with power and great glory" (Luke 21:27). One day we will walk in the Lord's presence and see the glory for ourselves. "For the Son of Man will come in the glory of His Father with His angels, and then He will reward each according to his works" (Matthew 16:27). Once the New Jerusalem is built there will be no need for the sun to illuminate those who live there, because the Son Himself, in His great glory, will be the light. What glory!

Prayer and God's Word is the Answer to Our Situation Today

This interesting prayer was given in Kansas, USA, at the opening session of their Senate. The prayer was given by minister Joel Wright. Here is the prayer: "*Heavenly Father, we come before you today to ask your forgiveness and to seek your direction and guidance.*

1. *We have lost our spiritual equilibrium and reversed our values.*
2. *We have ridiculed the absolute truth of Your Word and called it pluralism.*
3. *We have worshiped other gods and called it multiculturalism.*
4. *We have endorsed perversion and called it an alternate lifestyle.*
5. *We have exploited the poor and called it the lottery.*
6. *We have rewarded laziness and called it welfare.*
7. *We have killed our unborn and called it a choice.*
8. *We have shot abortionists and called it justifiable.*
9. *We have neglected to discipline our children and called it building self-esteem.*
10. *We have abused power and called it politics.*
11. *We have embezzled public funds and called it essential expenses.*
12. *We have institutionalized bribery and called it suites of office.*
13. *We have coveted our neighbors' possessions and called it ambition.*

14. We have polluted the air with profanity and pornography and called it freedom of expression.
15. We have ridiculed the time-honored values of our forefathers and called it enlightenment.

Search us, O God, and know our hearts today."

When this prayer was released, the Central Christian Church in Kansas logged more than 5,000 phone calls with only forty-seven being negative. The church is now receiving requests for this prayer from around the world.

> IT IS A TIME FOR SPIRITUAL FITNESS, PRAYER, AND THE POWER OF HOPE.

Luke 1:37—NOTHING IS IMPOSSIBLE WITH GOD. The word "nothing" is used seventy-five times in the New Testament and has twelve different meanings. The meaning in Luke 1:37 is the Greek word rhema which, as mentioned before, is the word for the revealed Word of God (John 15:7). This is the only place in the New Testament where the word nothing is rhema—impossible (impotent or weak). We all know that without faith it is impossible to please God (Hebrews 11:6).

In my new book, *Your Body is God's Temple*, I deal with prayer in Chapter 5. Here is a summary of the chapter:

1. Eighteen important prayer-preparation principles.
2. The importance of praising God in prayer.
3. Five important biblical principles on waiting for God.
4. Stand in faith, even when you are having the hardest time of your life.
5, Twelve principles of Solomon's prayer in dedicating the Temple when God's glory filled the air.

6. My belief is that if we follow the Scriptural instruction and examples for prayer, we will experience God's glory again.

The King is Coming. Are You Ready?
(1 Thessalonians 4:13-18)

This is one of the mysteries (1 Corinthians 15:51-58).

Shalom, Barry Borthistle.

THE BLOOD OF JESUS CHRIST IS THE MOST POWERFUL FORCE IN THE ENTIRE UNIVERSE
—Charles Spurgeon and David Wilkinson

We celebrate this awesome truth of what Christ did for us, including:

1. Salvation
2. Healing
3. Spiritual Authority

We celebrate this incredible truth through communion, but communion should not be rushed (1 Corinthians 11:17-34).

In the Old Testament, the High Priest would offer a perfect lamb, which was bred and born in Bethlehem, for the atonement of their sins. This would be celebrated once per year, known as the Day of Atonement or Yom Kippur.

In the Old Testament, the word atonement is mentioned about 80 times. In the New Testament, it is mentioned only once (Romans 5:11). The word atonement in the New Testament means "divine blessing."

In the Old Testament, the high priest was the only one that had access to God, that being on Yom Kippur.

In the New Testament, Jesus Christ is our High Priest, and we have access to him 24/7 (Hebrews 4:12-14). Jesus Christ was the perfect lamb who died for us, who was also born in Bethlehem. Think about this when you celebrate communion.

Jesus Paid it All

God is not obligated to bring victory to the rebellious or the disobedient unless sin is repented (1 John 1:5-10).

THE KING IS COMING. ARE YOU READY? (1 THESSALONIANS 4:13-18)

Spiritual Tip:

Fast and pray once a week, or every day if the Lord instructs you, and take communion as often as desired. There is nothing in Scripture to indicate that communion must be served by a priest or pastor or elder.

A COMMUNION PRAYER

1. Lord Jesus, I bow before you in humility and ask you to examine my heart today. Show me anything that is not pleasing to you. Reveal any secret pride, any unconfessed sin, any rebellion or unforgiveness that may be hindering my relationship with you. The price you paid covered me for all time, and my desire is to live for you.

2. As I take the bread representing your body that was broken for me, I remember and celebrate your faithfulness to me and to all who will receive you. I cannot begin to fathom the agonizing suffering of your crucifixion. Yet you took that pain for me and died for me. Thank you, Jesus. Thank you for your extravagant love and unmerited favor.

3. As I take the cup, representing your blood which was poured out from a splintered cross, I realize that you were the supreme sacrifice for all my sin, past, present, and future. Because of your blood shed for me, and your body broken for me, I can be free from the penalty of sin. Today, I remember and celebrate the precious gift of life that you gave me through your spilled blood.

4. Each time I take communion, Lord, I want to recommit my life, my heart, my thoughts, my everything to you. Fill me today with the power of the Holy Spirit. As I go on my way today, please help me to hold this fresh remembrance and the complete story of salvation that never grows old. Help me to share this message faithfully, as you give me opportunity, with others. I ask this in the precious name of Jesus Christ the Messiah and the soon-coming King.

Book Coming Soon Teaching in Detail All the 33 Things the Holy Spirit Does for Us

This is Awesome

1. He helps us (Romans 8:26).
2. He guides us (John 16:13).
3. He teaches us (John 14:26).
4. He speaks (Revelation 2:7).
5. He reveals (1 Corinthians 2:10).
6. He instructs (Acts 8:26-29).
7. He testifies of Jesus Christ (John 15:26).
8. He comforts us (Acts 9:31).
9. He calls us (Acts 13:4-12).
10. He fills us (Acts 4:31).
11. He strengthens us (Ephesians 3:16).
12. He prays for us (Romans 8: 26).
13. He prophecies through us (2 Peter 1:21).
14. He bears witness to the truth (Romans 9:1).
15. He brings joy (1 Thessalonians 1:6).
16. He brings freedom (2 Corinthians 3:17).
17. He helps us to obey (1 Peter 1:22).
18. He calls for the Return of Jesus (Revelation 22:17).
19. He transforms us (2 Corinthians 3:18).
20. He lives in us (1 Corinthians 3:16-17).
21. He frees us (Romans 8:2).
22. He renews us (Titus 3:5).
23. He produces fruit in us (Galatians 5:22-23).
24. He gives us spiritual gifts (1 Corinthians 12:8-10).
25. He leads us (Romans 8:14).
26. He convicts us of sin (John 16:8).

27. He sends for us (2 Thessalonians 2:13).
28. He empowers us (Acts 1:8).
29. He unites us (Ephesians 4:3-4).
30. He seals us (Ephesians 1:13).
31. He gives us access to the Father (Ephesians 2:18).
32. He enables us to wait (Galatians 5:5).
33. He casts out demons (Matthew 12:28).

—Courtesy of *Charisma* Magazine

> We need the Holy Spirit to help us maintain our Spiritual Authority

Remember this:

1. We are the Temple of the Holy Spirit (1 Corinthians 3:16-17; 6:17-20).
2. The Holy Spirit is God and it is very important that we do not grieve Him but please Him (Ephesians 4:25-32).
3. Walk in love (Ephesians 5:1-7).
4. Walk in light (Ephesians 5:8-14).
5. Walk in wisdom (Ephesians 5:15-21).

Consider the Seven Key Principles to become Your Declaration of Intent

1. Your body is the Temple of the Holy Spirit (1 Corinthians 3:16-17, 6:17-20). Spiritual Authority begins with our recognition of this principle.
2. Be certain that the Holy Spirit lives within you by repenting of your sins, and accepting Jesus Christ as your personal savior (John 3:15-21).

THE 33 THINGS THE HOLY SPIRIT DOES FOR US

3. The Holy Spirit is God, and desires a personal relationship with us (Ephesians 4:23-32).
4. God responds to four major obedience principles:

   1. Repentance. We are told in Scripture that our repentance can actually have God change His mind. Examples: Jonah, Moses, Amos.
   2. Obedience (1 Samuel 15:22-23).
   3. Faith. Without faith it is impossible (impotent) to please God (Hebrews 11:6).
   4. Praise. The Lord considers praise as a New Testament sacrifice (Hebrews 13:15). David tells us that God inhabits or dwells in the praises of His people. This is another reason why we must walk and live as God's Temple.

5. When we understand Spiritual Authority, God gives us the opportunity to ask Him to supply our needs (John 15:1-11). Two key words in this passage:

   1. Abide which means "to dwell".
   2. If (our choice) we abide in the word we may ask what we desire (word – rhema, which means revealed, or it becomes ALIVE).

6. The greatest way to praise the Lord is to say, "HALLELUJAH," which means joyously praising Him. Interesting point! As far as I know, hallelujah is pronounced exactly the same in every language on the face of the Earth.
7. The power of prayer (Philippians 4:4-9).

Even *The Wall Street Journal* agrees with the Bible:

"For societies founded on biblical traditions, pandemics need not make for the end. This is a call for repentance and revival. Great struggles can produce great clarity."

In the Old Testament, it would seem that men of spiritual resources may not only redeem catastrophe but turn the moment into a great creative opportunity."

I challenge all of us to take up this opportunity. Shalom,

Barry Borthistle 604- 761-3281
bborthistle@shaw.ca
www.solomonsporchteaching.com

God Bless All of You

About the Author

Barry C. Borthistle has led six different companies or organizations to the multi-million-dollar sales category. He has accomplished this in different sectors of retail and direct sales, both as an owner and as corporate leader. He is cofounder of TriVita, Inc., a global wellness company.

Barry is a great motivator, leadership teacher, and growth expert for individuals and organizations. He is married to Ruth, who is the love of his life, with five children, fifteen grandchildren, and five great-grandchildren. He resides in Vancouver, British Columbia, Canada.

BUSINESS BACKGROUND

- Former president of a 200-million-dollar nutritional company, Enrich International.
- Fifteen years climbing the corporate executive ladder with The Bay, Sears, and Canadian Tire.

- Thirty years self-employed, owned or began several small businesses in the retail sector and in the direct-selling industry.
- Cofounder and former President of The TriVita Way International, 1999-2007.
- Six years as a pastor, Calvary Chapel.
- Currently, Presidential Director at TriVita, Inc.

AWARDS

- The Price-Waterhouse Recognition for New Start-up companies, 1996.
- The prestigious Winston Churchill Award, 1997.
- Featured in North America's "Who's Who in Business", 1998, 2004.
- Leading Health Professionals of the World, 2006.
- Entrepreneurial Leadership Award, 2008, Trinity Western University, Langley, British Columbia.
- Cofounder Award, TriVita, 2012.
- Invited by Queen Elizabeth on the Royal Yacht Britannia in Boston Harbor to discuss business opportunities in the UK.

EDUCATION

- BA in Marketing

Author of *Your Body is God's Temple*

"Here is My Dream…

My Dream is to achieve or develop a worldwide movement that encourages people to understand and live like their body is the Temple of God.

'Dream A Dream so big that if God is not in it, it will fail"

—Hudson Taylor

Excerpt from "The Unshakeable Truth" by Josh McDowell:

"Do we really know who we are and the authority that we have in and through Jesus Christ?

Life requires vast amounts of information…The key feature to life is information. Life, even the simplest of bacterial cells, requires vast amounts of information to function. Cellular information is stored in DNA. The DNA in one cell in the human body holds the equivalent of roughly 8,000 books of information. A typical human body has about 100 trillion cells, each of which has a DNA strand that could be uncoiled to about three meters in length. Thus, if the DNA in an adult human were strung together, it would stretch from earth to the sun and back around seventy times!"